Witness for the Prosecution

A PLAY IN THREE ACTS

by Agatha Christie

SAMUEL FRENCH, INC.

45 WEST 25TH STREET   NEW YORK 10010
7623 SUNSET BOULEVARD   HOLLYWOOD 90046
LONDON   *TORONTO*

WITNESS FOR THE PROSECUTION

Produced by Peter Saunders at The Winter Garden Theatre, London, on the 28th October 1953, with the following cast of characters:

(in the order of their appearance)

GRETA, typist to Sir Wilfred .... *Rosalie Westwater*
CARTER, Sir Wilfred's Chief Clerk ... *Walter Horsbrugh*
MR. MAYHEW, a solicitor .... *Milton Rosmer*
LEONARD VOLE .... *Derek Blomfield*
SIR WILFRED ROBARTS, Q.C. .... *David Horne*
INSPECTOR HEARNE .... *David Raven*
PLAIN-CLOTHES DETECTIVE .... *Kenn Kennedy*
ROMAINE .... *Patricia Jessel*
CLERK OF THE COURT .... *Philip Holles*
MR. JUSTICE WAINWRIGHT .... *Percy Marmont*
ALDERMAN .... *Walter Horsbrugh*
MR. MYERS, Q.C. .... *D. A. Clarke-Smith*
COURT USHER .... *Nicolas Tannar*
COURT STENOGRAPHER .... *John Bryning*
WARDER .... *Denzil Ellis*
THE JUDGE'S CLERK .... *Muir Little*
1ST BARRISTER .... *George Dudley*
2ND BARRISTER .... *Jack Bulloch*
3RD BARRISTER ....*Lionel Gadsden*
4TH BARRISTER .... *John Farries Moss*
5TH BARRISTER .... *Richard Coke*
6TH BARRISTER .... *Agnes Fraser*
1ST MEMBER OF THE JURY .... *Lauderdale Beckett*
2ND MEMBER OF THE JURY .... *Iris Fraser Foss*
3RD MEMBER OF THE JURY .... *Kenn Kennedy*
A POLICEMAN .... *David Homewood*
DR. WYATT, a police surgeon .... *Graham Stuart*
JANET MACKENZIE .... *Jean Stuart*
MR. CLEGG, a laboratory assistant ...... *Peter Franklin*
THE OTHER WOMAN .... *Rosemary Wallace*

The play directed by Wallace Douglas

Décor by Michael Weight

Suggestions for reducing the cast to ten men and five women will be found on page 7.

SYNOPSIS OF SCENES

ACT ONE

The Chambers of Sir Wilfrid Robarts, Q.C. Afternoon.

ACT TWO

The Central Criminal Court, London—better known as the Old Bailey. Six weeks later. Morning.

ACT THREE

SCENE I. The chambers of Sir Wilfrid Robarts, Q.C. The same evening.

SCENE II: The Old Bailey. The next morning.

During Act Three, Scene II, the lights are lowered to denote the passing of one hour.

Copy of program for the first performance of WITNESS
FOR THE PROSECUTION as produced at Henry Miller's
Theatre, New York, December 16, 1954.

Gilbert Miller and Peter Saunders

present

WITNESS FOR THE PROSECUTION

A Murder Mystery by
Agatha Christie

Production directed by Robert Lewis with

Francis L. Sullivan   Patricia Jessel
Ernest Clark   Gene Lyons
Una O'Connor   Robin Craven   Horace Braham

Production designed by Raymond Sovey

Costumes supervised by Kathryn Miller

CAST

(In order of appearance)

CARTER .... *Gordon Nelson*
GRETA .... *Mary Barclay*
SIR WILFRID ROBARTS, Q.C. .... *Francis L. Sullivan*
MR. MAYHEW .... *Robin Craven*
LEONARD VOLE .... *Gene Lyons*
INSPECTOR HEARNE .... *Claude Horton*
PLAIN CLOTHES DETECTIVE .... *Ralph Leonard*
ROMAINE .... *Patricia Jessel*
THIRD JUROR .... *Dolores Rashid*
SECOND JUROR .... *Andrew George*
FOREMAN OF THE JURY .... *Jack Bittner*
COURT USHER .... *Arthur Oshlag*
CLERK OF THE COURT .... *Ronald Dawson*
MR. MYERS, Q.C. .... *Ernest Clark*
MR. JUSTICE WAINWRIGHT .... *Horace Braham*
ALDERMAN .... *R. Cobden-Smith*

JUDGE'S CLERK .... *Harold Webster*
COURT STENOGRAPHER .... *W. H. Thomas*
WARDER .... *Ralph Roberts*
BARRISTER .... *Henry Craig Neslo*
BARRISTER .... *..Brace Conning*
BARRISTER .... *Ruth Greene*
BARRISTER .... *Albert Richards*
BARRISTER .... *Franklyn Monroe*
BARRISTER .... *Sam Kramer*
POLICEMAN .... *Bryan Herbert*
DR. WYATT .... *Guy Spaull*
JANET MACKENZIE .... *Una O'Connor*
MR. CLEGG .... *Michael McAloney*
THE OTHER WOMAN .... *Dawn Steinkamp*

SYNOPSIS OF SCENES

ACT ONE

The chambers of Sir Wilfrid Robarts, Q.C., in London.
Late afternoon.

ACT TWO

The Central Criminal Court (The Old Bailey) in London.
Morning. Six weeks later.

ACT THREE

SCENE I: The chambers of Sir Wilfrid Robarts, Q.C., in
London. The same evening.
SCENE II: The Old Bailey. The next morning.

(The lights will be lowered during this scene to denote
the passing of one hour.)

TIME: The present.
Production stage manager, JOHN EFFRAT

AUTHOR'S NOTE

I have great faith in the ingenuity of amateurs and repertory companies to devise means of reducing the very large cast of *Witness for the Prosecution* in order to make it possible to perform, and my suggested means of reducing the cast is probably only one of many.

As there are a large number of non-speaking parts, it may well be that local amateurs can be used, or members of the audience be invited on to the stage, and I believe that this would be greatly to the benefit of the play rather than lose the spectacle of a lot of people in the court scene.

Although Greta never appears at the same time as "The Other Woman," i.e. the strawberry blonde in the final scene, this part should *not* be doubled, as the audience will think it is "plot"—which, of course, it isn't.

The play has given me enormous enjoyment in writing, and I do hope that the repertory companies who do it will derive the same pleasure from it. Good luck.

AGATHA CHRISTIE

CARTER	Can double the Judge
INSPECTOR HEARNE	Can double Policeman at end of last act
PLAIN-CLOTHES DETECTIVE	Can be doubled by Warder
CLERK OF THE COURT	This part can be combined with Court Usher
ALDERMAN	Can be dispensed with
COURT STENOGRAPHER	Can be dispensed with
JUDGE'S CLERK	Can be dispensed with
SIX BARRISTERS	Four can be dispensed with
THREE MEMBERS OF THE JURY	These can be dispensed with and the "taking of the oath" and "returning the verdict" can be done by a voice "off"
MR. MYERS, Q.C.	Can double plain-clothes Detective

7

Witness for the Prosecution

ACT ONE

SCENE: *The chambers of Sir Wilfrid Robarts, Q.C.*

The scene is Sir Wilfrid's private office. It is a narrow room with the door L. and a window R. The window has a deep built-in window seat and over-looks a tall plain brick wall. There is a fireplace C. of the back wall, flanked by bookcases filled with heavy legal volumes. There is a desk R.C. with a swivel chair R. of it and a leather-covered upright chair L. of it. A second upright chair stands against the bookcases L. of the fireplace. In the corner up R. is a tall reading desk, and in the corner up L. are some coat-hooks attached to the wall. At night the room is lit by electric candle-lamp wall-brackets R. and L. of the fireplace and an angle-poise lamp on the desk. The light switch is below the door L. There is a bell push L. of the fireplace. The desk has a telephone on it and is littered with legal documents. There are the usual deed-boxes and there is a litter of documents on the window seat.

(See the Ground Plan and Photograph of the Scene.)

When the Curtain rises it is afternoon and there is sun-shine streaming in through the window R. The office is empty. GRETA, *Sir Wilfrid's typist, enters immedi-ately. She is an adenoidal girl with a good opinion of herself. She crosses to the fireplace, doing a "square dance" step, and takes a paper from a box-file on the mantelpiece.* CARTER, *the Chief Clerk, enters. He carries some letters.* GRETA *turns, sees* CARTER, *crosses and quietly exits.* CARTER *crosses to the desk and puts the letters on it. The TELEPHONE rings.* CARTER *lifts the receiver.*

CARTER. *(Into the telephone.)* Sir Wilfrid Robart's Chambers . . . Oh, it's you, Charles . . . No, Sir Wilfrid's in Court . . . Won't be back just yet . . . Yes, Shuttleworth Case . . . What—with Myers for the prosecution and Banter trying it? . . . He's been giving judgment for close on two hours already . . . No, not an earthly this evening. We're full up. Can give you an appointment tomorrow . . . No, couldn't possibly. I'm expecting Mayhew, of Mayhew and Brinskill you know, any minute now . . . Well, so long. *(He replaces the receiver and sorts the documents on the desk.)*

GRETA. *(Enters. She is painting her nails.)* Shall I make the tea, Mr. Carter?

CARTER. *(Looking at his watch)* It's hardly time yet, Greta.

GRETA. It is by my watch.

CARTER. Then your watch is wrong.

GRETA. *(Crossing to C.)* I put it right by the radio.

CARTER. Then the radio must be wrong.

GRETA. *(Shocked.)* Oh, not the radio, Mr. Carter. That *couldn't* be wrong.

CARTER. This watch was my father's. It never gains nor loses. They don't make watches like that nowadays. *(He shakes his head, then suddenly changes his manner and picks up one of the typewritten papers.)* Really, your typing. Always mistakes. *(He crosses to R. of* GRETA.*)* You've left out a word.

GRETA. Oh, well—just one word. Anyone might do that.

CARTER. The word you have left out is the word *not.* The omission of it entirely alters the sense.

GRETA. Oh, does it? That's rather funny when you come to think of it. *(She giggles.)*

CARTER. It is not in the least funny. *(He tears the letter in half and hands the piece to her.)* Do it again. You may remember I told you last week about the celebrated case of Bryant and Horsfall. Case of a will and a trust fund, and entirely owing to a piece of careless copying by a clerk . . .

GRETA. *(Interrupting)* The wrong wife got the money, I remember.

CARTER. A woman divorced fifteen years previously. Absolutely contrary to the intention of the testator, as his lordship himself admitted. But the wording had to stand. They couldn't do anything about it. *(He crosses above the desk to R. of it.)*

GRETA. I think *that's* rather funny, too. *(She giggles.)*

CARTER. Counsel's Chambers are no place to be funny in. The Law, Greta, is a serious business and should be treated accordingly.

GRETA. You wouldn't think so—to hear some of the jokes Judges make.

CARTER. That kind of joke is the prerogative of the Bench.

GRETA. And I'm always reading in the paper about "laughter in Court."

CARTER. If that's not caused by one of the Judge's remarks you'll find he'll soon threaten to have the Court cleared.

GRETA. *(Crossing to the door)* Mean old thing. *(She turns and crosses to L. of the desk.)* Do you know what I read the other day, Mr. Carter. *(Sententiously.)* "The Law's an Ass." I'm not being rude. It's a quotation.

CARTER. *(Coldly.)* A quotation of a facetious nature. Not meant to be taken seriously. *(He looks at his watch.)* You can make the tea— *(He pauses, waiting for the exact second.)* —now, Greta.

GRETA. *(Gladly.)* Oh, thank you, Mr. Carter. *(She crosses quickly to the door.)*

CARTER. Mr. Mayhew, of Mayhew and Brinskill, will

be here shortly. A Mr. Leonard Vole is also expected. They may come together or separately.

GRETA. *(Excitely.)* Leonard Vole? *(She crosses to the desk.)* Why, that's the name—it was in the paper . . .

CARTER. *(Repressively.)* The tea, Greta.

GRETA. Asked to communicate with the police as he might be able to give them useful information.

CARTER. *(Raising his voice)* Tea!

GRETA. *(Crossing to the door and turning)* It was only last . . .

(CARTER *glowers at* GRETA.)

The tea, Mr. Carter. (GRETA, *abashed but unsatisfied, exits.)*

CARTER. *(Continues his arrangement of the papers, muttering to himself.)* These girls. Sensational—inaccurate— I don't know what the Temple's coming to. *(He examines a typewritten document, makes an angry sound, picks up a pen and makes a correction.)*

GRETA. *(Enters. Announcing)* Mr. Mayhew.

(MR. MAYHEW *and* LEONARD VOLE *enter.* MAYHEW *is a typical middle-aged solicitor, shrewd and rather dry and precise in manner.* LEONARD *is a likeable, friendly young man, about twenty-seven. He is looking faintly worried.* MAYHEW *carries a brief-case.)*

MAYHEW. *(Giving his hat to* GRETA) Sit down, Mr. Vole. *(He crosses and stands above the desk.)* Good afternoon, Carter. *(He puts his brief-case on the desk.)*

(GRETA *takes* LEONARD'S *hat and hangs both on the pegs above the door. She then exits, staring at* LEONARD *over her shoulder.)*

CARTER. Good afternoon, Mr. Mayhew. Sir Wilfrid shouldn't be long, sir, although you never can tell with Mr. Justice Banter. I'll go straight over to the Robing Room and tell him that you're here— *(He hesitates.)* with . . . *(He crosses below the desk to* R. *of* LEONARD.)

MAYHEW. With Mr. Leonard Vole. Thank you, Carter. I'm afraid our appointment was at rather short notice. But in this case time is—er—rather urgent.

(CARTER *crosses to the door.*)

How's the lumbago?

CARTER. *(Turning)* I only feel it when the wind is in the East. Thank you for remembering, Mr. Mayhew. (CARTER *exits hurriedly.*)

(MAYHEW *sits* L. *of the desk.* LEONARD *prowls uneasily.*)

MAYHEW. Sit down, Mr. Vole.

LEONARD. Thanks—I'd rather walk about. I—this sort of thing makes you feel a bit jumpy. *(He crosses down* L.)

MAYHEW. Yes, yes, very probably . . .

GRETA. *(Enters. She speaks to* MAYHEW, *but stares with fascinated interest at* LEONARD.) Would you care for a cup of tea, Mr. Mayhew? I've just made it.

LEONARD. *(Appreciatively.)* Thanks. I don't mind if I . . .

MAYHEW. *(Interrupting; decisively.)* No, thank you.

(GRETA *turns to exit.*)

LEONARD. *(To* GRETA.) Sorry. *(He smiles at her.)*

(GRETA *smiles at* LEONARD *and exits. There is a pause.*)

(He crosses up R. *Abruptly and with a rather likeable air of bewilderment.)* What I mean is, I can't believe it's *me* this is happening to. I keep thinking—perhaps it's all a dream and I'll wake up presently.

MAYHEW. Yes, I suppose one might feel like that.

LEONARD. *(Moving to* R. *of the desk)* What I mean is —well, it seems so silly.

MAYHEW. *(Sharply.)* Silly, Mr. Vole?

LEONARD. Well, yes. I mean I've always been a friendly sort of chap—get on with people and all that. I mean, I'm not the sort of fellow that does—well, anything violent.

(He pauses.) But I suppose it will be—all right, won't it?
I mean you don't get convicted for things you haven't
done in this country, do you?

MAYHEW. Our English judicial system is, in my opinion,
the finest in the world.

LEONARD. *(Is not much comforted. Crossing above the
desk to* L.) Of course there was that case of—what was
his name—Adolf Beck. I read about it only the other day.
After he'd been in prison for years, they found out it was
another chap called Smith. They gave him a free pardon
then. That's a thing that seems odd to me— giving you a
"pardon" for something you haven't done.

MAYHEW. It is the necessary legal term.

LEONARD. *(Bringing the chair from* L. *of the fireplace
and setting it* C.) Well, it doesn't seem right to me.

MAYHEW. The important thing was that Beck was set
at liberty.

LEONARD. Yes, it was all right for him. But if it had
been murder now— *(He sits astride the chair* C.) if it had
been murder it would have been too late. He would have
been hanged.

MAYHEW. *(Dry but kindly.)* Now, Mr. Vole, there is
really no need to take a—er—morbid point of view.

LEONARD. *(Rather pathetically.)* I'm sorry, sir. But
you see, in a way, I'm rather getting the wind up.

MAYHEW. Well, try and keep calm. Sir Wilfrid Robarts
will be here presently and I want you to tell your story
to him exactly as you told it to me.

LEONARD. Yes, sir.

MAYHEW. But meantime perhaps we might fill out a
little more of the detail—er—background. You are at
present, I understand, out of a job?

LEONARD. *(Embarrassed.)* Yes, but I've got a few
pounds put by. It's not much, but if you can see your
way . . .

MAYHEW. *(Upset.)* Oh, I'm not thinking of—er—legal
fees. It's just the—er—pictures I'm trying to get clear.
Your surroundings and—er—circumstances. How long
have you been unemployed?

LEONARD. *(Answers everything readily, with an engaging friendliness.)* About a couple of months.

MAYHEW. What were you doing before that?

LEONARD. I was in a motor servicing firm—kind of mechanic, that's what I was.

MAYHEW. How long had you worked there?

LEONARD. Oh, about three months.

MAYHEW. *(Sharply.)* Were you discharged?

LEONARD. No, I quit. Had words with the foreman. Proper old b— *(He breaks off.)* That is, he was a mean sort of chap, always picking on you.

MAYHEW. Hm! And before that?

LEONARD. I worked in a petrol station, but things got a bit awkward and I left.

MAYHEW. Awkward? In what way?

LEONARD. *(Embarrassed.)* Well—the boss's daughter— she was only a kid, but she took a—well, a sort of fancy to me—and there was nothing there shouldn't have been between us, but the old man got a bit fed up and said I'd better go. He was quite nice about it and gave me a good chit. *(He rises and suddenly grins.)* Before *that*, I was selling egg beaters on commission. *(He replaces the chair* L. *of the fireplace.)*

MAYHEW. Indeed.

LEONARD. *(Crossing and standing above the desk: boyishly.)* And a rotten job they were, too. I could have invented a better egg beater myself. *(Catching* MAYHEW's *mood)* You're thinking I'm a bit of a drifter, sir. It's true in a way—but I'm not really like that. Doing my army service unsettled me a bit—that and being abroad. I was in Germany. It was fine there. That's where I met my wife. She's an actress. Since I've come back to this country I can't seem somehow to settle down properly. I don't know really just what I want to do—I like working on cars best and thinking out new gadgets for them. That's interesting, that is. And you see . . .

(SIR WILFRID ROBARTS, Q.C., *enters. He is followed on by* CARTER. SIR WILFRID *is wearing his Q.C.'s jacket*

and bands and carries his wig and gown. CARTER
carries SIR WILFRID'S *ordinary jacket and bow tie.)*

SIR WILFRID. Hullo, John.

MAYHEW. *(Rising)* Ah, Wilfrid.

SIR WILFRID. *(Handing the wig and gown to* CARTER*)*
Carter told you I was in Court? Banter really surpassed
himself. *(He looks at* LEONARD.*)* And this is Mr.—er—
Vole? *(He crosses to* L. *of* LEONARD.*)*

MAYHEW. This is Leonard Vole.

LEONARD. How do you do, sir?

(MAYHEW *moves to the fireplace.)*

SIR WILFRID. How do you do, Vole? Won't you sit
down?

(LEONARD *sits* L. *of the desk.)*

How's the family, John? *(He crosses to* CARTER.*)*

(CARTER *assists* SIR WILFRID *to change his jacket and
remove his bands.)*

MAYHEW. Molly's got a touch of this twenty-four hour
flu.

SIR WILFRID. Too bad!

MAYHEW. Yes, damnable. Did you win your case, Wilfrid?

SIR WILFRID. Yes, I'm glad to say.

MAYHEW. It always gives you satisfaction to beat
Myers, doesn't it?

SIR WILFRID. It gives me satisfaction to beat anyone.

MAYHEW. But especially Myers.

SIR WILFRID. *(Taking the bow tie from* CARTER*)* Especially Myers. *(He crosses to the mirror* R.*)* He's an
irritating—gentleman. *(He puts on his bow tie.)* He
always seems to bring out the worst in me.

MAYHEW. That would appear to be mutual. You irri-
tate him because you hardly ever let him finish a sentence.

(CARTER *exits, taking the wig, gown, jacket and bands
with him.*)

SIR WILFRID. He irritates me because of that manner-
ism of his. *(He turns and stands* R. *of the desk.)* It's this—
(He clears his throat and adjusts an imaginary wig.) that
drives me to distraction, and he will call me Ro-barts—
Ro-barts. But he's a very able advocate, if only he'd
remember not to ask leading questions when he knows
damn well he shouldn't. But let's get down to business.

MAYHEW. *(Moving above the desk)* Yes. I brought
Vole here, because I am anxious for you to hear his story
exactly as he told it to me. *(He takes some typewritten
papers from his brief-case.)* There is some urgency in the
matter, it seems. *(He hands the papers to* SIR WILFRID.)

SIR WILFRID. Oh?

LEONARD. My wife thinks I'm going to be arrested.
(He looks embarrassed.) She's much cleverer than I am—
so she may be right.

SIR WILFRID. Arrested for what?

LEONARD. *(Still more embarrassed.)* Well—for murder.

(SIR WILFRID *perches himself on the down* R. *corner of
the desk.*)

MAYHEW. *(Crossing to* C.) It's the case of Miss Emily
French. You've probably seen the reports in the Press?
    (SIR WILFRID *nods.*)
She was a maiden lady, living alone but for an elderly
housekeeper, in a house at Hampstead. On the night of
October the fourteenth her housekeeper returned at eleven
o'clock to find that apparently the place had been broken
into, and that her mistress had been coshed on the back
of the head and killed. *(To* LEONARD.) That is right?

LEONARD. That's right. It's quite an ordinary sort of
thing to happen nowadays. And then, the other day, the
papers said that the police were anxious to interview a
Mr. Leonard Vole, who had visited Miss French earlier
on the evening in question, as they thought he might be

able to give them useful information. So of course I went along to the police station and they asked me a lot of questions.

SIR WILFRID. *(Sharply.)* Did they caution you?

LEONARD. *(Vaguely.)* I don't quite know. I mean they said would I like to make a statement and they'd write it down, and it might be used in Court. Is that cautioning me?

(SIR WILFRID *exchanges a glance with* MAYHEW, *and speaks more to him than to* LEONARD.)

SIR WILFRID. *(Rising)* Oh well, can't be helped now. *(He crosses above the desk to* L.)

LEONARD. Anyway, it sounded damned silly to me. I told them all I could and they were very polite and seemed quite satisfied and all that. When I got home and told Romaine about it—my wife that is—well, she got the wind up. She seemed to think that they—well—that they'd got hold of the idea that *I* might have done it.

(SIR WILFRID *moves the chair from* L. *of the fireplace to* C. *for* MAYHEW, *who sits.*)

So I thought perhaps I ought to get hold of a solicitor— *(To* MAYHEW.) so I came along to you. I thought you'd be able to tell me what I ought to do about it. *(He looks anxiously from one to the other.)*

SIR WILFRID. *(Moving down* L.) You knew Miss French well?

(LEONARD *rises, but* SIR WILFRID *motions him to sit.)*

LEONARD. Oh yes, she'd been frightfully kind to me. *(He resumes his seat.)* Actually it was a bit of a bore sometimes—she positively fussed over me, but she meant it very well, and when I saw in the paper that she'd been killed I was awfully upset, because, you see, I'd really got fond of her.

MAYHEW. Tell Sir Wilfrid, just as you told me, how it was you came to make Miss French's acquaintance.

LEONARD. *(Turning obediently to* SIR WILFRID*)* Well, it was one day in Oxford Street. I saw an old lady crossing the road carrying a lot of parcels and in the middle of the street she dropped them, tried to get hold of them again and found a bus was almost on top of her.

(SIR WILFRID *crosses slowly below the* OTHERS *to* R. *of desk.)*

Just managed to get to the curb safely. Well, I recovered her parcels from the street, wiped some of the mud off them as best I could, tied up one again that had burst open with string and generally soothed the old dear down. You know the sort of thing.

SIR WILFRID. And she was grateful?

LEONARD. Oh yes, she seemed very grateful. Thanked me a lot and all that. Anyone would think I'd saved her life instead of her parcels.

SIR WILFRID. There was actually no question of your having saved her life? *(He takes a packet of cigarettes from the desk drawer.)*

LEONARD. Oh, no. Nothing heroic. I never expected to see her again.

SIR WILFRID. Cigarette?

LEONARD. No, thanks, sir, never do. But by an extraordinary coincidence, two days later I happened to be sitting behind her in the theatre. She looked round and recognized me and we began to talk, and in the end she asked me to come and see her.

SIR WILFRID. And you went?

LEONARD. Yes. She'd urged me to name a day specially and it seemed rather churlish to refuse. So I said I'd go on the following Saturday.

SIR WILFRID. And you went to her house at . . . *(He looks at one of the papers.)*

MAYHEW. Hampstead.

LEONARD. Yes.

SIR WILFRID. What did you know about her when you first went to the house? *(He perches himself on the down* R. *corner of the desk.)*

LEONARD. Well, nothing really but what she'd told me,

that she lived alone and hadn't very many friends. Something of that kind.

SIR WILFRID. She lived with only a housekeeper?

LEONARD. That's right. She had eight cats, though. Eight of them. The house was beautifully furnished and all that, but it smelt a bit of cat.

SIR WILFRID. *(Rising and moving above the desk)* Had you reason to believe she was well off?

LEONARD. Well, she talked as though she was.

SIR WILFRED. And you yourself? *(He crosses and stands up L. of LEONARD.)*

LEONARD. *(Cheerfully.)* Oh, I'm practically stony broke and have been for a long time.

SIR WILFRID. Unfortunate.

LEONARD. Yes, it is rather. Oh, you mean people will say I was sucking up to her for her money?

SIR WILFRID. *(Disarmed.)* I shouldn't have put it quite like that, but in essence, yes, that is possibly what people might say.

LEONARD. It isn't really true, you know. As a matter of fact, I was sorry for her. I thought she was lonely. I was brought up by an old aunt, my Aunt Betsy, and I like old ladies.

SIR WILFRID. You say old ladies. Do you know what age Miss French was?

LEONARD. Well, I didn't know, but I read it in the paper after she murdered. She was fity-six.

SIR WILFRID. Fifty-six. You consider that old, Mr. Vole, but I should doubt if Miss Emily French considered herself old.

LEONARD. But you can't call it a chicken, can you?

SIR WILFRID. *(Crossing above the desk and sitting R. of it)* Well, let us get on. You went to see Miss French fairly frequently?

LEONARD. Yes, I should say once, twice a week perhaps.

SIR WILFRID. Did you take your wife with you?

LEONARD. *(Slightly embarrassed.)* No, no, I didn't.

SIR WILFRID. Why didn't you?

LEONARD. Well—well, frankly, I don't think it would have gone down very well if I had.

SIR WILFRID. Do you mean with your wife or with Miss French?

LEONARD. Oh, with Miss French. *(He hesitates.)*

MAYHEW. Go on, go on.

LEONARD. You see, she got rather fond of me.

SIR WILFRID. You mean, she fell in love with you?

LEONARD. *(Horrified.)* Oh, good Lord no, nothing of that kind. Just sort of pampered me and spoiled me, that sort of thing.

SIR WILFRID. *(After a short pause.)* You see, Mr. Vole, I have no doubt part of the police case against you, if there *is* a case against you which as yet we have no definite reason to suppose, will be why did you, young, good-looking, married, devote so much of your time to an elderly woman with whom you could hardly have very much in common?

LEONARD. *(Gloomily.)* Yes, I know they'll say I was after her for her money. And in a way perhaps that's true. But only in a way.

SIR WILFRED. *(Slightly disarmed.)* Well, at least you're frank, Mr. Vole. Can you explain a little more clearly?

LEONARD. *(Rising and moving to the fireplace)* Well, she made no secret of the fact that she was rolling in money. As I told you, Romaine and I—that's my wife—are pretty hard up. *(He moves and stands above his chair.)* I'll admit that I did hope that if I was really in a tight place she'd lend me some money. I'm being honest about it.

SIR WILFRID. Did you ask her for a loan?

LEONARD. No, I didn't. I mean, things weren't desperate. *(He becomes suddenly rather more serious as though he realized the gravity of that.)* Of course I can see—it does look rather bad for me. *(He resumes his seat.)*

SIR WILFRID. Miss French knew you were a married man?

LEONARD. Oh, yes.

SIR WILFRID. But she didn't suggest that you should bring your wife to see her?

LEONARD. *(Slightly embarrassed.)* No. She—well, she seemed to take it for granted my wife and I didn't get on.

SIR WILFRID. Did you deliberately give her that impression?

LEONARD. No, I didn't. Indeed I didn't. But she seemed to—well, assume it, and I thought perhaps if I kept dragging Romaine into it she'd well, lose interest in me. I didn't want exactly to cadge money from her, but I'd invented a gadget for a car—a really good idea it is—and if I could have persuaded her to finance that, well, I mean it would have been *her* money, and it might have brought her in a lot. Oh, it's very difficult to explain—but I wasn't sponging on her, Sir Wilfrid, really I wasn't.

SIR WILFRID. What sums of money did you obtain at any time from Miss French?

LEONARD. None. None at all.

SIR WILFRID. Tell me something about the housekeeper.

LEONARD. Janet MacKenzie? She was a regular old tyrant, you know, Janet was. Fairly bullied poor Miss French. Looked after her very well and all that, but the poor old dear couldn't call her soul her own when Janet was about. *(Thoughtfully.)* Janet didn't like me at all.

SIR WILFRID. Why didn't she like you?

LEONARD. Oh, jealous, I expect. I don't think she liked my helping Miss French with her business affairs.

SIR WILFRID. Oh, so you helped Miss French with her business affairs?

LEONARD. Yes. She was worried about some of her investments and things, and she found it a bit difficult to fill up forms and all that sort of thing. Yes, I helped her with a lot of things like that.

SIR WILFRID. Now, Mr. Vole, I'm going to ask you a very serious question. And it's one to which it's vital I should have a truthful answer. You were in low water financially, you had the handling of this lady's affairs.

Now did you at any time convert to your own use the securities that you handled?

(LEONARD *is about to repudiate this hotly.*)

Now, wait a minute, Mr. Vole, before you answer. Because, you see, there are two points of view. Either we can make a feature of your probity and honesty or, if you swindled the woman in any way, then we must take the line that you had no motive for murder, since you had already a profitable source of income. You can see that there are advantages in either point of view. What I want is the truth. Take your time if you like before you reply.

LEONARD. I assure you, Sir Wilfrid, that I played dead straight and you won't find anything to the contrary. Dead straight.

SIR WILFRID. Thank you, Mr. Vole. You relieve my mind very much. I pay you the compliment of believing that you are far too intelligent to lie over such a vital matter. And we now come to October the . . . *(He hesitates.)*

MAYHEW. The fourteenth.

SIR WILFRID. Fourteenth. *(He rises.)* Did Miss French ask you to go and see her that night?

LEONARD. No, she didn't, as a matter of fact. But I'd come across a new kind of gadget and I thought she'd like it. So I slipped up there that evening and got there about a quarter to eight. It was Janet MacKenzie's night out and I knew she'd be alone and might be rather lonely.

SIR WILFRID. It was Janet MacKenzie's night out and you knew that fact.

LEONARD. *(Cheerfully.)* Oh yes, I knew Janet always went out on a Friday.

SIR WILFRID. That's not quite so good.

LEONARD. Why not? It seems very natural that I should choose that evening to go and see her.

SIR WILFRID. Please go on, Mr. Vole.

LEONARD. Well, I got there at a quarter to eight. She'd finished her supper but I had a cup of coffee with her and we played a game of Double Demon. Then at nine o'clock I said good night to her and went home.

(SIR WILFRID *crosses below the* OTHERS *to* L.)

MAYHEW. You told me the housekeeper said she came home that evening earlier than usual.

LEONARD. Yes, the police told me she came back for something she'd forgotten and she heard—or she says she heard—somebody talking with Miss French. Well, whoever it was, it wasn't me.

SIR WILFRID. Can you prove that, Mr. Vole?

LEONARD. Yes, of course I can prove it. I was at home again with my wife by then. That's what the police kept asking me. Where I was at nine-thirty. Well, I mean some days one wouldn't know where one was. As it happens I can remember quite well that I'd gone straight home to Romaine and we hadn't gone out again.

SIR WILFRID. *(Crossing up* C.) You live in a flat?

LEONARD. Yes. We've got a tiny maisonette over a shop behind Euston Station.

SIR WILFRID. *(Standing up* L. *of* LEONARD) Did anybody see you returning to the flat?

LEONARD. I don't suppose so. Why should they?

SIR WILFRID. It might be an advantage if they had.

LEONARD. But surely you don't think—I mean if she were really killed at half past nine my wife's evidence is all I need, isn't it?

(SIR WILFRID *and* MAYHEW *look at each other.* SIR WILFRID *crosses and stands* L.)

MAYHEW. And your wife will say definitely that you were at home at that time?

LEONARD. Of course she will.

MAYHEW. *(Rising and moving to the fireplace)* You are very fond of your wife and your wife is very fond of you?

LEONARD. *(His face softening)* Romaine is absolutely devoted to me. She's the most devoted wife any man could have.

MAYHEW. I see. You are happily married.

LEONARD. Couldn't be happier. Romaine's wonderful,

absolutely wonderful. I'd like you to know her, Mr. Mayhew.

(There is a KNOCK at the door.)

SIR WILFRID. *(Calling)* Come in.

GRETA. *(Enters. She carries an evening paper.)* The evening paper, Sir Wilfrid. *(She points to a paragraph as she hands the paper to him.)*

SIR WILFRID. Thank you, Greta.

GRETA. Would you like a cup of tea, sir?

SIR WILFRED. No, thank you. Oh, would you like a cup, Vole?

LEONARD. No, thank you, sir.

SIR WILFRID. No, thank you, Greta. *(He crosses below the OTHERS to R. of the desk)*

(GRETA exits.)

MAYHEW. I think it would be advisable for us to have a meeting with your wife.

LEONARD. You mean have a regular round-table conference?

(SIR WILFRID sits R. of the desk.)

MAYHEW. I wonder, Mr. Vole, if you are taking this business quite seriously enough?

LEONARD. *(Nervously.)* I am. I am, really, but it seems —well, I mean it seems so much like a bad dream. I mean that it should be happening to me. Murder. It's a thing you read about in books or newspapers, but you can't believe it's a thing that could ever happen to you, or touch you in any way. I suppose that's why I keep trying to make a joke of it, but it isn't a joke, really.

MAYHEW. No, I'm afraid it's not a joke.

LEONARD. But I mean it's all right, isn't it? Because I mean if they think Miss French was killed at half past nine and I was at home with Romaine . . .

MAYHEW. How did you go home? By bus or under-ground?

LEONARD. I walked. It took me about twenty-five min-utes, but it was a fine night—a bit windy.

MAYHEW. Did you see anyone you knew on the way?

LEONARD. No, but does it matter? I mean Romaine . . .

SIR WILFRID. The evidence of a devoted wife unsup-ported by any other evidence may not be completely con-vincing, Mr. Vole.

LEONARD. You mean, they'd think Romaine would tell a lie on my accocnt?

SIR WILFRID. It has been known, Mr. Vole.

LEONARD. Oh, I'm sure she would, too, only in this case I mean she won't be telling a lie. I mean it really is so. You do believe me, don't you?

SIR WILFRID. Yes, I believe you, Mr. Vole, but it's not me you will have to convince. You are aware, are you not, that Miss French left a will leaving you all her money?

LEONARD. (Absolutely flabbergasted.) Left all her money to me? You're joking!

(MAYHEW resumes his seat c.)

SIR WILFRID. I'm not joking. It's in tonight's evening paper. (He hands the paper across the desk.)

LEONARD. (Reads the paragraph.) Well, I can hardly believe it.

SIR WILFRID. You knew nothing about it?

LEONARD. Absolutely nothing. She never said a word. (He hands the paper to MAYHEW.)

MAYHEW. You're quite sure of that, Mr. Vole?

LEONARD. Absolutely sure. I'm very grateful to her—yet in a way I rather wish now that she hadn't. I mean it —it's a bit unfortunate as things are, isn't it, sir?

SIR WILFRID. It supplies you with a very adequate motive. That is, if you knew about it, which you say you didn't. Miss French never talked to you about making a will?

LEONARD. She said to Janet once, "You're afraid I shall

make my will again," but that was nothing to do with me. I mean, it was just a bit of a dust-up between them. *(His manner changes.)* Do you really think they're going to arrest me?

SIR WILFRID. I think you must prepare yourself, Mr. Vole, for that eventuality.

LEONARD. *(Rising)* You—you will do the best you can for me, won't you, sir?

SIR WILFRID. *(With friendliness.)* You may rest assured, my dear Mr. Vole, that I will do everything in my power to help you. Don't worry. Leave everything in my hands.

LEONARD. You'll look after Romaine, won't you? I mean, she'll be in an awful state—it will be terrible for her.

SIR WILFRID. Don't worry, my boy. Don't worry.

LEONARD. *(Resuming his seat; to* MAYHEW.) Then the money side, too. That worries me. I've got a few quid, but it's not much. Perhaps I oughtn't to have asked you to do anything for me.

MAYHEW. I think we shall be able to put up adequate defence. The Court provides for these cases, you know.

LEONARD. *(Rising and moving above the desk)* I can't believe it. I can't believe that I, Leonard Vole, may be standing in a dock saying "Not guilty." People staring at me. *(He shakes himself as though it were a bad dream then turns to* MAYHEW.) I can't see why they don't think it was a burglar. I mean, apparently the window was forced and smashed and a lot of things were strewn around, so the papers said. *(He resumes his seat.)* I mean, it seems much more probable.

MAYHEW. The police must have some good reason for not thinking that it was a burglary.

LEONARD. Well, it seems to me . . .

(CARTER *enters.*)

SIR WILFRID. Yes, Carter?

CARTER. *(Crossing above the desk)* Excuse me, sir, there are two gentlemen here asking to see Mr. Vole.

SIR WILFRID. The police?

CARTER. Yes, sir.

(MAYHEW *rises.*)

SIR WILFRID. *(Rising and crossing to the door)* All right, John, I'll go and talk to them.

(SIR WILFRID *exits and* CARTER *follows him off.*)

LEONARD. My God! Is this—it?

MAYHEW. I'm afraid it may be, my boy. Now take it easy. Don't lose heart. *(He pats* LEONARD *on the shoulder.)* Make no further statement—leave it all to us. *(He replaces his chair* L. *of the fireplace.)*

LEONARD. But how did they know I'm here?

MAYHEW. It seems probable that they have had a man watching you.

LEONARD. *(Still unable to believe it.)* Then they really do suspect me.

(SIR WILFRID, DETECTIVE INSPECTOR HEARNE *and a plainclothe* DETECTIVE *enter. The* INSPECTOR *is a tall, good-looking officer.)*

INSPECTOR. *(As he enters; to* SIR WILFRID.) I'm sorry to trouble you, sir.

SIR WILFRID. *(Standing up* L.) This is Mr. Vole.

(LEONARD *rises.*)

INSPECTOR. *(Crossing to* LEONARD) Is your name Leonard Vole?

LEONARD. Yes.

INSPECTOR. I am Detective Inspector Hearne. I have here a warrant for your arrest on the charge of murdering Emily French on October fourteenth last. I must warn you that anything you say may be taken down and used in evidence.

LEONARD. O.K. *(He looks nervously at* SIR WILFRID *then crosses and takes his hat from the hooks up* L.) I'm ready.

MAYHEW. *(Moving to* L. *of the* INSPECTOR) Good afternoon, Inspector Hearne. My name is Mayhew. I am representing Mr. Vole.

INSPEDTOR. Good afternoon, Mr. Mayhew. That's quite all right. We'll take him along and charge him now.

*(*LEONARD *and the* DETECTIVE *exit.)*

(He crosses to SIR WILFRID. *To* MAYHEW.) Very seasonable weather we're having just now. Quite a nip of frost last night. We'll be seeing you later, sir, I expect. *(He crosses to the door.)* Hope we haven't inconvenienced you, Sir Wilfrid.

SIR WILFRID. I am never inconvenienced.

*(*THE INSPECTOR *laughs politely and exits.)*

(He closes the door.) I must say, John, that that young man is in a worse mess than he seems to think.

MAYHEW. He certainly is. How does he strike you?

SIR WILFRID. *(Crossing to* L. *of* MAYHEW) Extraordinarily naïve. Yet in some ways quite shrewd. Intelligent, I should say. But he certainly doesn't realize the danger of his position.

MAYHEW. Do you think he did it?

SIR WILFRID. I've no idea. On the whole, I should say *not. (Sharply.)* You agree?

MAYHEW. *(Taking his pipe from his pocket)* I agree.

*(*SIR WILFRID *takes the tobacco jar from the mantelpiece and hands it to* MAYHEW, *who crosses, stands above the desk and fills his pipe.)*

SIR WILFRID. Oh well, he seems to have impressed both of us favourably. I can't think why. I never heard a weaker story. God knows what we're going to do with it. The only evidence in his favour seems to be his wife's—and who's going to believe a wife?

MAYHEW. *(With dry humour.)* It has been known to happen.

SIR WILFRID. She's a foreigner, too. Nine out of the twelve in a jury box believe a foreigner is lying anyway. She'll be emotional and upset, and won't understand what the prosecuting counsel says to her. Still, we shall have to interview her. You'll see, she'll have hysterics all over my Chambers.

MAYHEW. Perhaps you'd prefer not to accept the brief.

SIR WILFRID. Who says I won't accept it? Just because I point out that the boy has an absolute tomfool story to tell.

MAYHEW. *(Crossing and handing the tobacco jar to* SIR WILFRID) But a true one.

SIR WILFRID. *(Replacing the jar on the mantelpiece)* It must be a true one. It couldn't be so idiotic if it wasn't true. Put all the facts down in black and white and the whole thing is utterly damning.

(MAYHEW *feels in his pockets for matches.)*
And yet, when you talk to the boy, and he blurts out these damning facts, you realize that the whole thing could happen just as he said. Damn it, I had the equivalent of an Aunt Betsy myself. I loved her dearly.

MAYHEW. He's got a good personality, I think. Sympathetic.

SIR WILFRID. *(Taking a matchbox from his pocket and handing it to* MAYHEW) Yes, he ought to go down well with the jury. That cuts no ice with the Judge, though. And he's the simple sort of chap who may get rattled easily in the box.

(MAYHEW *finds that the box is empty and throws it in the waste-paper basket.)*
A lot depends on this girl.
(There is a KNOCK at the door.)
(He calls.) Come in.

(GRETA *enters. She is excited and a little scared. She closes the door.)*
Yes, Greta, what is it?

GRETA. *(In a whisper.)* Mrs. Leonard Vole is here.

MAYHEW. Mrs. Vole.

SIR WILFRID. Come here. You saw that young man? He's been arrested for murder.

GRETA. *(Crossing to L. of SIR WILFRID)* I know. Isn't it exciting?

SIR WILFRID. Do you think he did it?

GRETA. Oh no, sir, I'm sure he didn't.

SIR WILFRID. Oh, why not?

GRETA. He's far too nice.

SIR WILFRID. *(To MAYHEW.)* That makes three of us. *(To GRETA.)* Bring Mrs. Vole in.

(GRETA *crosses and exits.*)

And we're probably three credulous fools— *(He crosses to the chair L. of the desk.)* taken in by a young man with a pleasing personality. *(He sets the chair in readiness for* ROMAINE.)

CARTER. *(Enters and stands to one side. Announcing)* Mrs. Vole.

(ROMAINE *enters. She is a foreign woman of great personality, but very quiet. Her voice has a strangely ironic inflection.*)

MAYHEW. *(Crossing to R. of ROMAINE)* My dear Mrs. Vole. *(He goes towards her with a great air of sympathy, but is slightly rebuffed by her personality.)*

(CARTER *exits, closing the door behind him.*)

ROMAINE. Ah! You are Mr. Mayhew.

MAYHEW. Yes. This is Sir Wilfrid Robarts, who has agreed to handle your husband's case for him.

ROMAINE. *(Crossing to C.)* How do you do, Sir Wilfrid?

SIR WILFRID. How do you do?

ROMAINE. I have just come from your office, Mr. Mayhew. They told me you were here with my husband.

SIR WILFRID. Quite, quite.

ROMAINE. Just as I arrived I thought I saw Leonard getting into a car. There were two men with him.

SIR WILFRID. Now, my dear Mrs. Vole, you must not upset yourself.

(ROMAINE *is not in the least upset.*)

(He is slightly disconcerted.) Won't you sit down, here?

ROMAINE. Thank you. *(She sits in the chair L. of the desk.)*

SIR WILFRID. *(Moving above the desk to R. of it)* There is nothing to be alarmed about as yet, and you must not give way. *(He moves below the desk.)*

ROMAINE. *(After a pause.)* Oh, no, I shall not give way.

SIR WILFRID. Then let me tell you that, as perhaps you already suspect, your husband has just been arrested.

ROMAINE. For the murder of Miss Emily French?

SIR WILFRID. I'm afraid so, yes. But please don't be upset.

ROMAINE. You keep saying that, Sir Wilfrid, but I am not upset.

SIR WILFRID. No. No, I see you have great fortitude.

ROMAINE. You can call it that if you like.

SIR WILFRID. The great thing is to be calm and to tackle all this sensibly.

ROMAINE. That suits me very well. But you must not hide anything from me, Sir Wilfrid. You must not try and spare me. I want to know everything. *(With a slightly different inflection.)* I want to know—the worst.

SIR WILFRID. Splendid. Splendid. That's the right way to tackle things. *(He moves to R. of the desk.)* Now, dear lady, we're not going to give way to alarm or despondency, we're going to look at things in a sensible and straightforward manner. *(He sits R. of the desk.)* Your husband became friendly with Miss French about six weeks ago. You were—er—aware of that friendship?

ROMAINE. He told me that he had rescued an old lady and her parcels one day in the middle of a crowded street. He told me that she had asked him to go and see her.

SIR WILFRID. All very natural, I think. And your husband did go and see her.

ROMAINE. Yes.

SIR WILFRID. And they became great friends.

ROMAINE. Evidently.

SIR WILFRID. There was no question of your accompanying your husband on any occasion?

ROMAINE. Leonard thought it better not.

SIR WILFRID. *(Shooting a keen glance at her)* He thought it better not. Yes. Just between ourselves, why did he think it better not?

ROMAINE. He thought Miss Frnech would prefer it that way.

SIR WILFRID. *(A little nervously and sliding off the subject.)* Yes, yes, quite. Well, we can go into that some other time. Your husband, then, became friends with Miss French, he did her various little services, she was a lonely old woman with time on her hands and she found your husband's companionship congenial to her.

ROMAINE. Leonard can be very charming.

SIR WILFRID. Yes, I'm sure he can. He felt, no doubt, it was a kindly action on his part to go and cheer up the old lady.

ROMAINE. I daresay.

SIR WILFRID. You yourself did not object at all to your husband's friendship with this old lady?

ROMAINE. I do not think I objected, no.

SIR WILFRID. You have, of course, perfect trust in your husband, Mrs. Vole. Knowing him as well as you do . . .

ROMAINE. Yes, I know Leonard very well.

SIR WILFRID. I can't tell you how much I admire your calm and your courage, Mrs. Vole. Knowing as I do how devoted you are to him . . .

ROMAINE. So you know how devoted I am to him?

SIR WILFRID. Of course.

ROMAINE. But excuse me, I am a foreigner. I do not always know your English terms. But is there not a saying about knowing something of your own knowledge?

You do not know that I am devoted to Leonard, of your own knowledge, do you, Sir Wilfrid? *(She smiles.)*

SIR WILFRID. *(Slightly disconcerted.)* No, no, that is of course true. But your husband told me.

ROMAINE. Leonard told you how devoted I was to him?

SIR WILFRID. Indeed, he spoke of your devotion in the most moving terms.

ROMAINE. Men, I often think, are very stupid.

SIR WILFRID. I beg your pardon?

ROMAINE. It does not matter. Please go on.

SIR WILFRID. *(Rising and crossing above the desk to c.)* This Miss French was a woman of some considerable wealth. She had no near relations. Like many eccentric elderly ladies she was fond of making wills. She had made several wills in her lifetime. Shortly after meeting your husband she made a fresh will. After some small bequests she left the whole of her fortune to your husband.

ROMAINE. Yes.

SIR WILFRID. You know that?

ROMAINE. I read it in the paper this evening.

SIR WILFRID. Quite, quite. Before reading it in the paper, you had no idea of the fact? Your husband had no idea of it?

ROMAINE. *(After a pause.)* Is that what he told you?

SIR WILFRID. Yes. You don't suggest anything different?

ROMAINE. No. Oh, no. I do not suggest anything.

SIR WILFRID. *(Crossing above the desk to R. of it and sitting)* There seems to be no doubt that Miss French looked upon your husband rather in the light of a son, or perhaps a very favourite nephew.

ROMAINE. *(With distinct irony.)* You think Miss French looked upon Leonard as a son?

SIR WILFRID. *(Flustered.)* Yes, I think so. Definitely I think so. I think that could be regarded as quite natural, quite normal under the circumstances.

ROMAINE. What hypocrites you are in this country.

(MAYHEW *sits on the chair* L. *of the fireplace.*)

SIR WILFRID. My dear Mrs. Vole!

ROMAINE. I shock you? I am so sorry.

SIR WILFRID. Of course, of course. You have a continental way of looking at these things. But I assure you, dear Mrs. Vole, that is *not* the line to take. It would be most unwise to suggest in any way that Miss French had —er—any—er—feelings for Leonard Vole other than those of a—of a mother or—shall we say—an aunt.

ROMAINE. Oh, by all means let us say an aunt, if you think it best.

SIR WILFRID. One has to think of the effect on the jury of all these things, Mrs. Vole.

ROMAINE. Yes. I also wish to do that. I have been thinking of that a good deal.

SIR WILFRID. Quite so. We must work together. Now we come to the evening of October fourteenth. That is just over a week ago. You remember that evening?

ROMAINE. I remember it very well.

SIR WILFRID. Leonard Vole called on Miss French that evening. The housekeeper, Janet MacKenzie, was out. Mr. Vole played a game of Double Demon with Miss French and finally took leave of her about nine o'clock. He returned home on foot, he tells me, arriving at approximately twenty-five minutes past nine. *(He looks interrogatively at her.)*

(ROMAINE *rises and moves to the fireplace.* SIR WILFRID *and* MAYHEW *rise.*)

ROMAINE. *(Without expression; thoughtfully.)* Twenty-five past nine.

SIR WILFRID. At half past nine the housekeeper returned to the house to get something she had forgotten. Passing the sitting-room door she heard Miss French's voice in conversation with a man. She assumed that the man with Miss French was Leonard Vole, and Inspector Hearne says that it is this statement of hers which has

led to your husband's arrest. Mr. Vole, however, tells
me that he has an absolute alibi for that time, since he was
at home with you at nine-thirty.

(There is a pause. ROMAINE *does not speak although*
SIR WILFRID *looks at her.)*

That is so, is it not? He was with you at nine-thirty?

(SIR WILFRID *and* MAYHEW *look at* ROMAINE.)

ROMAINE. That is what Leonard says? That he was
home with me at nine-thirty?

SIR WILFRID. *(Sharply.)* Isn't it true?

(There is a long silence.)

ROMAINE. *(Moving to the chair* L. *of the desk; presently.)* But of course. *(She sits.)*

SIR WILFRID. *(Sighs with relief and resumes his seat*
R. *of the desk.)* Possibly the police have already questioned you on that point?

ROMAINE. Oh yes, they came to see me yesterday evening.

SIR WILFRID. And you said . . .?

ROMAINE. *(As though repeating something that she has
learned by rote)* I *said* Leonard came in at nine-twenty-
five that night and did not go out again.

MAYHEW. *(A little uneasily.)* You said . . .? Oh!
(He sits on the chair L. *of the fireplace.)*

ROMAINE. That was right, was it not?

SIR WILFRID. What do you mean by that, Mrs. Vole?

ROMAINE. *(Sweetly.)* That is what Leonard wants me
to say, is it not?

SIR WILFRID. It's the truth. You said so just now.

ROMAINE. I have to understand—to be sure. If I say
yes, it is so, Leonard was with me in the flat at nine-
thirty—will they acquit him?

(SIR WILFRID *and* MAYHEW *are puzzled by* RO-
MAINE'S *manner.)*

Will they let him go?

MAYHEW. *(Rising and crossing to* L. *of her)* If you are both speaking the truth then they will—er—have to acquit him.

ROMAINE. But when I said—that—to the police, I do not think they believed me. *(She is not distressed; instead she seems faintly satisfied.)*

SIR WILFRID. What makes you think they did not believe you?

ROMAINE. *(With sudden malice.)* Perhaps I did not say it very well?

(SIR WILFRID *and* MAYHEW *exchange glances.* MAYHEW *resumes his seat.* ROMAINE'S *cool, impudent glance meets* SIR WILFRID'S. *There is definite antagonism between them.)*

SIR WILFRID. *(Changing his manner)* You know, Mrs. Vole, I don't quite understand your attitude in all this.

ROMAINE. So you don't understand? Well, perhaps it is difficult.

SIR WILFRID. Perhaps your husband's position is not quite clear to you?

ROMAINE. I have already said that I want to understand fully just how black the case against—my husband is. I say to the police, Leonard was at home with me at nine-thirty—and they do not believe me. But perhaps there is someone who saw him leave Miss French's house, or who saw him in the street on his way home? *(She looks sharply and rather slyly from one to the other.)*

(SIR WILFRID *looks enquiringly at* MAYHEW.)

MAYHEW. *(Rising and moving* C.; *reluctantly.)* Your husband cannot think of, or remember, anything helpful of that kind.

ROMAINE. So it will be only his word—and mine. *(With intensity.)* And mine. *(She rises abruptly.)* Thank you, that is what I wanted to know. *(She crosses to* L.)*

MAYHEW. But, Mrs. Vole, please don't go. There is a lot more to be discussed.

ROMAINE. Not by me.

SIR WILFRID. Why not, Mrs. Vole?

ROMAINE. I shall have to swear, shall I not, to speak the truth and all the truth and nothing but the truth? *(She seems amused.)*

SIR WILFRID. That is the oath you take.

ROMAINE. *(Crossing and standing above the chair L. of the desk; now openly mocking)* And suppose that then, when you ask me —*(She imitates a man's voice.)* "When did Leonard Vole come home that night?" I should say . . .

SIR WILFRID. Well?

ROMAINE. There are so many things I could say.

SIR WILFRID. Mrs. Vole, do you love your husband?

ROMAINE. *(Shifting her mocking glance to MAYHEW)* Leonard says I do.

MAYHEW. Leonard Vole believes so.

ROMAINE. But Leonard is not very clever.

SIR WILFRID. You are aware, Mrs. Vole, that you cannot by law be called to give testimony damaging to your husband?

ROMAINE. How very convenient.

SIR WILFRID. And your husband can . . .

ROMAINE. *(Interrupting)* He is not my husband.

SIR WILFRID. What?

ROMAINE. Leonard Vole is not my husband. He went through a form of marriage with me in Berlin. He got me out of the Russian zone and brought me to this country. I did not tell him, but I had a husband living at the time.

SIR WILFRID. He got you out of the Russian sector and safely to this country? You should be very grateful to him. *(Sharply.)* Are you?

ROMAINE. One can get tired of gratitude.

SIR WILFRID. Has Leonard Vole ever injured you in any way?

ROMAINE. *(Scornfully.)* Leonard? Injured me? He worships the ground I walk on.

SIR WILFRED. And you?

(Again there is a duel of eyes between them, then she laughs and turns away.)

ROMAINE. You want to know too much. *(She crosses to the door.)*

MAYHEW. I think we must be quite clear about this. Your statements have been somewhat ambiguous. What exactly happened on the evening of October fourteenth?

ROMAINE. *(In a monotonous voice.)* Leonard came in at twenty-five minutes past nine and did not go out again. I have given him an alibi, have I not?

SIR WILFRID. *(Rising)* You have. *(He crosses to her.)* Mrs. Vole . . . *(He catches her eye and pauses.)*

ROMAINE. Yes?

SIR WILFRID. You're a very remarkable woman, Mrs. Vole.

ROMAINE. And you are satisfied, I hope? (ROMAINE *exits.)*

SIR WILFRID. I'm damned if I'm satisfied.

MAYHEW. Nor I.

SIR WILFRID. She's up to something, that woman—but what? I don't like it, John.

MAYHEW. She certainly hasn't had hysterics all over the place.

SIR WILFRID. Cool as a cucumber.

MAYHEW. *(Sitting on the chair L. of the desk)* What's going to happen if we put her into the witness box?

SIR WILFRID. *(Crossing to C.)* God knows!

MAYHEW. The prosecution would break her down in no time, especially if it were Myers.

SIR WILFRID. If it's not the Attorney-General, it probably will be.

MAYHEW. Then what's your line of attack?

SIR WILFRID. The usual. Keep interrupting—as many objections as possible.

MAYHEW. What beats me is that young Vole is convinced of her devotion.

SIR WILFRID. Don't put your trust in that. Any woman can fool a man if she wants to and if he's in love with her.

MAYHEW. He's in love with her all right. And trusts her completely.

SIR WILFRID. More fool he. Never trust a woman.

CURTAIN

ACT TWO

SCENE: *The Central Criminal Court, London—better known as the Old Bailey. Six weeks later. Morning.*

The section of the Court Room seen has a tall rostrum, the bench, running from down R. to up C. On it are the armchairs and desks for the Judge, his Clerk and the Alderman. Access to the bench is by a door in the up R. corner and by steps up R. from the floor of the court. On the wall over the Judge's chair are the Royal Arms and the Sword of Justice. Below the bench are small desks and chairs for the Clerk of the Court and the Court Stenographer. There is a small stool R. of the desks for the Usher. The witness box is immediately below the up C. end of the bench. Up C. is a door leading to the Barristers' robing room and up L.C. are glass-panelled double doors leading to a corridor and other parts of the building. Up L.C., between the doors, are two pews for the Barristers. Below the pews is a table with three chairs and a stool. The dock is L. and is entered by a door in the L. wall and a gate in the upstage rail. There are chairs in the dock for Leonard and the Warder. The jury box is down R., only the back of the three end seats being visible to the audience.

(See the Ground Plan and Photograph of Scene.)

When the Curtain rises, the Court has opened. The Judge, MR. JUSTICE WAINWRIGHT, *is seated* C. *of the bench. The* JUDGE'S CLERK *is seated* R. *of him and the* ALDERMAN *is seated* L. *of the Judge. The* CLERK OF THE COURT *and the* STENOGRAPHER *are in their seats below the bench.* MR. MYERS, Q.C., *for the Prosecu-*

*tion, is seated R. of the front row of Barristers with
his* ASSISTANT L. *of him.* SIR WILFRID, *for the Defence, is seated* L. *of the front row of Barristers with
his* AISSISTANT R. *of him. Four* BARRISTERS, *one a
woman, are seated in the back row of the Barristers'
seats.* LEONARD *is standing in the dock with the*
WARDER *beside him.* DR. WYATT *is seated on the
stool* R. *of the table. The* INSPECTOR *is seated on the
chair above the* R. *end of the table.* MAYHEW *is
seated* L. *of the table. A* POLICEMAN *stands at the
double doors. Three* MEMBERS *of the* JURY *are seen,
the first a man, the* FOREMAN, *the second a* WOMAN
and the third a MAN. *The* USHER *is administering
the oath to the* WOMAN JUROR *who is standing.*

WOMAN JUROR. *(Holding the Bible and oath card)*

. . . lady the Queen and the prisoner at the Bar whom
I shall have in charge, and a true verdict give according to
the evidence. *(She hands the Bible and oath card to the*
USHER, *then sits.)*

(The USHER *gives the Bible and oath card to the* FORE-
MAN.*)*

FOREMAN. *(Rising)* I swear by Almighty God that I
will well and truly try and true deliverance make between
our sovereign lady the Queen and the prisoner at the Bar
whom I shall have in charge, and a true verdict give
according to the evidence. *(He hands the Bible and oath
card to the* USHER, *then sits.)*

(The USHER *puts the Bible and card on the ledge of the
jury box, then sits on his stool down* R.*)*

CLERK. *(Rising)* Leonard Vole, you are charged on
indictment for that you on the fourteenth day of October
in the County of London murdered Emily Jane French.
How say you, Leonard Vole, are you guilty or not guilty?

LEONARD. Not guilty.

CLERK. Members of the Jury, the prisoner stands indicted for that he on the fourteenth day of October murdered Emily Jane French. To this indictment he has pleaded not guilty, and it is your charge to say, having heard the evidence, whether he be guilty or not. *(He motions to* LEONARD *to sit, then resumes his own seat.)*

*(*LEONARD *and the* WARDER *sit.* MYERS *rises.)*

JUDGE. One moment, Mr. Myers.

*(*MYERS *bows to the* JUDGE *and resumes his seat.)*
(He turns to the jury.) Members of the Jury, the proper time for me to sum up the evidence to you, and instruct you as to the law, is after you have heard all the evidence. But because there has been a considerable amount of publicity about this case in the Press, I would just like to say this to you now. By the oath which each of you has just taken you swore to try this case on the evidence. That means on the evidence that you are now going to hear and see. It does not mean that you are to consider also anything you have heard or read before taking your oaths. You must shut out from your minds everything except what will take place in this Court. You must not let anything else influence your minds in favour of or against the prisoner. I am quite sure that you will do your duty conscientiously in the way that I have indicated. Yes, Mr. Myers.

*(*MYERS *rises, clears his throat and adjusts his wig in the manner taken off by* SIR WILFRED *in the previous scene.)*

MYERS. May it please you, my lord. Members of the Jury, I appear in this case with my learned friend Mr. Barton for the prosecution, and my learned friends Sir Wilfrid Robarts and Mr. Brogan-Moore appear for the defence. This is a case of murder. The facts are simple and up to a certain point are not in dispute. You will hear how the prisoner, a young and, you may think, a not unattractive man, made the acquaintance of Miss Emily French, a woman of fifty-six. How he was treated by her with kindness and even with affection. The nature of that affection you will have to decide for yourselves. Dr. Wyatt will tell you that in his opinion death occurred at some time between nine-thirty and ten on the night of the fourteenth of October last. You will hear the evidence of Janet MacKenzie, who was Miss French's faithful and devoted housekeeper. The fourteenth of October—it was a Friday—was Janet MacKenzie's night out, but on this occasion she happened to return for a few minutes at nine twenty-five. She let herself in with a key and upon going upstairs to her room she passed the door of the sitting-room. She will tell you that in the sitting-room she heard the voices of Miss French and of the prisoner, Leonard Vole.

LEONARD. *(Rising)* That's not true. It wasn't me.

(The WARDER restrains LEONARD and makes him resume his seat.)

MYERS. Janet MacKenzie was surprised, since as far as she knew, Miss French had not expected Leonard Vole to call that evening. However, she went out again and when she returned finally at eleven she found Miss Emily French murdered, the room in disorder, a window smashed and the curtains blowing wildly. Horror-stricken, Janet MacKenzie immediately rang up the police. I should tell you that the prisoner was arrested on the twentieth of October. It is the case for the prosecution that Miss Emily Jane French was murdered between nine-thirty and ten p.m. on the evening of the fourteen of October, by a blow from a cosh and that the blow was struck by the prisoner. I will now call Inspector Hearne.

(The INSPECTOR rises. He holds a file of papers which he refers to often during the scene. He hands a type-written sheet to the CLERK and another to the

STENOGRAPHER. *He then enters the witness box. The*
CLERK *hands the sheet to the* JUDGE. *The* USHER
rises, crosses and stands by the witness box. The
INSPECTOR *picks up the oath card and Bible from
the ledge of the box.)*

INSPECTOR. I swear by Almighty God that the evidence
that I shall give shall be the truth, the whole truth and
nothing but the truth. Robert Hearne, Detective Inspector, Criminal Investigation Department, New Scotland Yard. *(He puts the Bible and oath card on the ledge
of the box.)*

(The USHER *crosses and sits on his stool.)*

MYERS. Now, Inspector Hearne, on the evening of the
fourteenth October last were you on duty when you received an emergency call?
INSPECTOR. Yes, sir.
MYERS. What did you do?
INSPECTOR. With Sergeant Randell I proceeded to
twenty-three Ashburn Grove. I was admitted to the house
and established that the occupant, whom I later ascertained was Miss Emily French, was dead. She was lying
on her face, and had received severe injuries to the back
of her head. An attempt had been made to force one of
th windows with some implement that might have been
a chisel. The window had been broken near the catch.
There was glass strewn about the floor, and I also later
found fragments of glass on the ground outside the window.
MYERS. Is there any particular significance in finding
glass both inside and outside the window?
INSPECTOR. The glass outside was not consistent with
the window having been forced from outside.
MYERS. You mean that if it had been forced from the
inside there had been an attempt to make it look as though
it had been done from the outside?
SIR WILFRID. *(Rising)* I object. My learned friend is

putting words into the witness's mouth. He really must observe the rules of evidence. *(He resumes his seat.)*

MYERS. *(To the* INSPECTOR.*)* You have been engaged on several cases of burglary and housebreaking?

INSPECTOR. Yes, sir.

MYERS. And in your experience when a window is forced from the outside, where is the glass?

INSPECTOR. On the inside.

MYERS. In any other case where the windows have been forced from the outside, have you found glass on the outside of the window some distance below, on the ground?

INSPECTOR. No.

MYERS. No. Will you go on?

INSPECTOR. A search was made, photographs were taken, the place was fingerprinted.

MYERS. What fingerprints did you discover?

INSPECTOR. Those of Miss Emily French herself, those of Janet MacKenzie and some which proved later to be those of the prisoner, Leonard Vole.

MYERS. No others?

INSPECTOR. No others.

MYERS. Did you subsequently have an interview with Mr. Leonard Vole?

INSPECTOR. Yes, sir. Janet MacKenzie was not able to give me his address, but as a result of a broadcast and a newspaper appeal, Mr. Leonard Vole came and saw me.

MYERS. And on October the twentieth, when arrested, what did the prisoner say?

INSPECTOR. He replied, "O. K. I'm ready."

MYERS. Now, Inspector, you say the room had the appearance of a robbery having been committed?

SIR WILFRED. *(Rising)* That is just what the Inspector did not say. *(To the* JUDGE.*)* If your lordship remembers, that was a suggestion made by my friend—and quite improperly made—to which I objected.

JUDGE. You are quite right, Sir Wilfrid.

    (MYERS *sits.*)

At the same time, I'm not sure that the Inspector is not entitled to give evidence of any facts which might tend to prove that the disorder of the room was not the work of a person who broke in from outside for the purpose of robbery.

SIR WILFRID. My lord, may I respectfully agree with what your lordship has said. Facts, yes. But not the mere expression of opinion without even the facts on which it is based. *(He sits.)*

MYERS. *(Rising)* Perhaps, my lord, if I phrased my question in this way my friend would be satisfied. Inspector, could you say from what you saw whether there had or had not been a bona fide breaking in from outside the house?

SIR WILFRID. *(Rising)* My lord, I really must continue my objection. My learned friend is again seeking to obtain an opinion from this witness. *(He sits.)*

JUDGE. Yes, Mr. Myers, I think you will have to do a little better than that.

MYERS. Inspector, did you find anything inconsistent with a breaking in from outside?

INSPECTOR. Only the glass, sir.

MYERS. Nothing else?

INSPECTOR. No, sir, there was nothing else.

JUDGE. We all seem to have drawn a blank there, Mr. Myers.

MYERS. Was Miss French wearing jewellery of any value?

INSPECTOR. She was wearing a diamond brooch, two diamond rings, value of about nine hundred pounds.

MYERS. And these were left untouched?

INSPECTOR. Yes, sir.

MYERS. Was in fact anything taken?

INSPECTOR. According to Janet MacKenzie, nothing was missing.

MYERS. In your experience, when anyone breaks into a house do they leave without taking anything?

INSPECTOR. Not unless they're interrupted, sir.

MYERS. But in this case it does not seem as if the burglar *was* interrupted.

INSPECTOR. No, sir.

MYERS. Do you produce a jacket, Inspector?
INSPECTOR. Yes, sir.

(The USHER *rises, crosses to the table, picks up the jacket
and hands it to the* INSPECTOR.)

MYERS. Is that it?
INSPECTOR. Yes, sir. *(He returns the jacket to the*
USHER.)

(The USHER *replaces the jacket on the table.)*

MYERS. From where did you get it?
INSPECTOR. I found it at the prisoner's flat some time
after he was arrested, and later handed it to Mr. Clegg
at the lab. to test for possible bloodstains.
MYERS. Lastly, Inspector, do you produce the will of
Miss French?

(The USHER *picks up the will from the table and hands
it to the* INSPECTOR.)

INSPECTOR. I do, sir.
MYERS. Dated October the eighth?
INSPECTOR. Yes, sir. *(He returns the will to the*
USHER.)

(The USHER *replaces the will on the table, crosses and
resumes his seat.)*

MYERS. After certain bequests, the residue is left to the
prisoner?
INSPECTOR. That's right, sir.
MYERS. And what is the net value of that estate?
INSPECTOR. It will be, as far as can be ascertained **at**
the moment, about eighty-five thousand pounds.

(MYERS *resumes his seat.* SIR WILFRID *rises.)*

SIR WILFRID. You say that the only fingerprints you found in the room were those of Miss French herself, the prisoner Leonard Vole and Janet MacKenzie. In your experience, when a burglar breaks in does he usually leave fingerprints or does he wear gloves?

INSPECTOR. He wears gloves.

SIR WILFRID. Invariably?

INSPECTOR. Almost invariably.

SIR WILFRID. So the absence of fingerprints in a case of robbery would hardly surprise you?

INSPECTOR. No, sir.

SIR WILFRID. Now, these chisel marks on the window. Where they on the inside or the outside of the casement?

INSPECTOR. On the outside, sir.

SIR WILFRID. Isn't that consistent—and only consistent—with a breaking in from the outside?

INSPECTOR. He could have gone out of the house afterwards to have done that, sir, or he could have made those marks from the inside.

SIR WILFRID. From the inside, Inspector? Now how could he have possibly done that?

INSPECTOR. There are two windows together there. Both are casements, and with their catches adjacent. It would have been easy for anyone in the room to open one window, lean out, and force the catch of the other.

SIR WILFRID. Tell me, did you find any chisel near the premises, or at the prisoner's flat?

INSPECTOR. Yes, sir. At the prisoner's flat.

SIR WILFRID. Oh?

INSPECTOR. But it didn't fit the marks on the window.

SIR WILFRID. It was a windy night, was it not, on October fourteenth?

INSPECTOR. I really can't remember, sir. *(He refers to his notes.)*

SIR WILFRID. According to my learned friend, Janet MacKenzie said that the curtains were blowing. Perhaps you noticed that fact yourself?

INSPECTOR. Well, yes, sir, they did blow about.

SIR WILFRID. Indicating that it was a windy night. I

suggest that if a burglar had forced the window from the outside and then swung it back, some of the loose glass might easily have fallen down *outside* the window, the window having been blown back violently by the wind. That is possible, is it not?

INSPECTOR. Yes, sir.

SIR WILFRID. Crimes of violence, as we all have been unhappily aware, have been much on the increase lately. You would agree to that, would you not?

INSPECTOR. It's been a little above normal, sir.

SIR WILFRID. Let us take the case that some young thugs had broken in, who meant to attack Miss French and steal; it is possible that if one of them coshed her and found that she was dead, they might give way to panic and leave without taking anything? Or they might even have been looking for money and would be afraid to touch anything in the nature of jewellery?

MYERS. *(Rising)* I submit that it is impossible for Inspector Hearne to guess at what went on in the minds of some *entirely* hypothetical young criminals who may not even exist. *(He sits.)*

SIR WILFRID. The prisoner came forward of his own accord and gave his statement quite willingly?

INSPECTOR. That is so.

SIR WILFRID. Is it the case that at all times the prisoner has protested his innocence?

INSPECTOR. Yes, sir.

SIR WILFRID. *(Indicating the knife on the table)* Inspector Hearne, will you kindly examine that knife?

   (The USHER *rises, crosses, picks up the knife and hands it to the* INSPECTOR.)

You have seen that knife before?

INSPECTOR. I may have.

SIR WILFRID. This is the knife taken from the kitchen table in Leonard Vole's flat and which was brought to your attention by the prisoner's wife on the occasion of your first interview with her.

MYERS. *(Rising)* My lord, to save the time of the Court, may I say that we accept this knife as being a knife in the possession of Leonard Vole and shown to the Inspector by Mrs. Vole. *(He sits.)*

SIR WILFRID. That is correct, Inspector?

INSPECTOR. Yes, sir.

SIR WILFRID. It is what is known, I believe, as a French vegetable knife?

INSPECTOR. I believe so, sir.

SIR WILFRID. Just test the edge of the knife with your finger—carefully.

(The INSPECTOR *tests the knife edge.)*

You agree that the cutting edge and the point are razor sharp?

INSPECTOR. Yes, sir.

SIR WILFRID. And if you were cutting—say, ham—carving it, that is, and your hand slipped with this knife, it would be capable of inflicting a very nasty cut, and one which would bleed profusely?

MYERS. *(Rising)* I object. That is a matter of opinion, and medical opinion at that. *(He sits.)*

(The USHER *takes the knife from the* INSPECTOR, *puts it on the table, crosses and resumes his seat.)*

SIR WILFRID. I withdraw the question. I will ask you instead, Inspector, if the prisoner, when questioned by you as to the stains on the sleeve of his jacket, drew your attention to a recently healed scar on his wrist, and stated that it had been caused by a household knife when he was slicing ham?

INSPECTOR. That is what he said.

SIR WILFRED. And you were told the same thing by the prisoner's wife?

INSPECTOR. The first time. Afterwards . . .

SIR WILFRID. *(Sharply.)* A simple yes or no, please. Did the prisoner's wife show you this knife, and tell you that her husband had cut his wrist with it slicing ham?

INSPECTOR. Yes, she did.

(SIR WILFRID resumes his seat.)

MYERS. *(Rising)* What first drew your attention to that jacket, Inspector?

INSPECTOR. The sleeve appeared to have been recently washed.

MYERS. And you were told this story about an accident with a kitchen knife?

INSPECTOR. Yes, sir.

MYERS. And your attention was drawn to a scar on the prisoner's wrist?

INSPECTOR. Yes, sir.

MYERS. Granted that that scar was made by this particular knife, there was nothing to show whether it was an accident or done deliberately?

SIR WILFRID. *(Rising)* Really, my lord, if my learned friend is going to answer his own questions, the presence of the witness seems to be superfluous. *(He sits.)*

MYERS. *(Resignedly.)* I withdraw the question. Thank you, Inspector.

(The INSPECTOR *stands down, crosses and exits up L. The* POLICEMAN *closes the door behind him.)*

Dr. Wyatt.

(DR. WYATT rises and enters the box. He carries some notes. The USHER rises, crosses, hands the Bible to him and holds up the oath card.)

WYATT. I swear by Almighty God that the evidence that I shall give shall be the truth, the whole truth and nothing but the truth.

(The USHER *puts the Bible and oath card on the ledge of the witness box, crosses and resumes his seat.)*

MYERS. You are Dr. Wyatt?

WYATT. Yes.

MYERS. You are a police surgeon attached to the Hampstead Division?

WYATT. Yes.

MYERS. Dr. Wyatt, will you kindly tell the Jury what

you know regarding the death of Miss Emily French?

WYATT. *(Reading from his notes)* At eleven p.m. on October fourteenth, I saw the dead body of the woman who subsequently proved to be Miss French. By examination of the body I was of the opinion that the death had resulted from a blow on the head, delivered from an object such as a cosh. Death would have been practically instantaneous. From the temperature of the body and other factors, I placed the time of death at not less than an hour previously and not more than, say, an hour and a half. That is to say between the hours of nine-thirty and ten p.m.

MYERS. Had Miss French struggled with her adversary at all?

WYATT. There was no evidence that she had done so. I should say, on the contrary, that she had been taken quite unprepared.

(MYERS *resumes his seat.*)

SIR WILFRID. *(Rising)* Doctor, where exactly on the head had this blow been struck? There was only one blow, was there not?

WYATT. Only one. On the left side at the asterion.

SIR WILFRID. I beg your pardon? Where?

WYATT. The asterion. The junction of the parietal, occipital and temple bones.

SIR WILFRID. Oh, yes. And in layman's language, where is that?

WYATT. Behind the left ear.

SIR WILFRID. Would that indicate that the blow had been struck by a left-handed person?

WYATT. It's difficult to say. The blow appeared to have been struck directly from behind, because the bruising ran perpendicularly. I should say it is really impossible to say whether it was delivered by a right- or left-handed man.

SIR WILFRID. We don't know yet that it was a *man*,

Doctor. But will you agree, from the position of the blow, that if anything it is more likely to have been delivered by a left-handed person?

WYATT. That is possibly so. But I would prefer to say that it is uncertain.

SIR WILFRID. At the moment the blow was struck, would blood have been likely to have got on to the hand or arm that struck the blow?

WYATT. Yes, certainly.

SIR WILFRID. And only on that hand or arm?

WYATT. Probably only on that hand and arm, but it's difficult to be dogmatic.

SIR WILFRID. Quite so, Doctor Wyatt. Now, would great strength have been needed to strike such a blow?

WYATT. No. From the position of the wound no great strength would have been needed.

SIR WILFRID. It would not necessarily be a man who had struck the blow. A woman could have done so equally well?

WYATT. Certainly.

SIR WILFRID. Thank you. *(He sits.)*

MYERS. *(Rising)* Thank you, Doctor. *(To the* USHER.*)* Call Janet MacKenzie.

(WYATT *stands down, crosses and exits up* L. *The* POLICE-MAN *opens the door. The* USHER *rises and crosses to* C.*)*

USHER. Janet MacKenzie.
POLICEMAN. *(Calling)* Janet MacKenzie.

(JANET MACKENZIE *enters up* L. *She is a tall, dour-looking Scotswoman. Her face is set in a grim line. Whenever she looks at* LEONARD, *she does so with loathing. The* POLICEMAN *closes the door.* JANET *crosses and enters the witness box. The* USHER *moves and stands beside the witness box.* JANET *picks up the Bible in her left hand.)*

USHER. Other hand, please. *(He holds out the oath card.)*

JANET. *(Puts the Bible into her right hand.)* I swear by Almighty God that the evidence that I shall give shall be the truth, the whole truth and nothing but the truth. *(She hands the Bible to the* USHER.)

(The USHER *puts the Bible and oath card on the ledge of the witness box, crosses and resumes his seat.)*

MYERS. Your name is Janet MacKenzie?

JANET. Aye—that's my name.

MYERS. You were companion housekeeper to the late Miss Emily French?

JANET. I was her housekeeper. I've no opinion of companions, poor feckless bodies, afraid to do a bit of honest domestic work.

MYERS. Quite so, quite so, I meant only that you were held in esteem and affection by Miss French, and were on friendly terms together. Not quite those of mistress and servant.

JANET. *(To the* JUDGE.) Twenty years I've been with her and looked after her. She knew me and she trusted me, and many's the time I've prevented her doing a foolish action!

JUDGE. Miss MacKenzie, would you please address your remarks to the Jury.

MYERS. What sort of a person was Miss French?

JANET. She was a warm-hearted body—too warm-hearted at times, I'm thinking. A wee bit impulsive too. There was times when she'd have no sense at all. She was easily flattered, you see.

MYERS. When did you first see the prisoner, Leonard Vole?

JANET. He came to the house, I mind, at the end of August.

MYERS. How often did he come to the house?

JANET. To begin with once a week, but later it was oftener. Two and even three times he'd come. He'd sit there flattering her, telling her how young she looked and noticing any new clothes she was wearing.

MYERS. *(Rather hastily.)* Quite, quite. Now will you tell the Jury in your own words, Miss MacKenzie, about the events of October the fourteenth.

JANET. It was a Friday and my night out. I was going round to see some friends of mine in Glenister Road, which is not above three minutes' walk. I left the house at half past seven. I'd promised to take my friend the pattern of a knitted cardigan that she'd admired. When I got there I found I'd left it behind, so after supper I said I'd slip back and get it as it was a fine night and no distance. I got back to the house at twenty-five past nine. I let myself in with my key and went upstairs to my room. As I passed the sitting-room door I heard the prisoner in there talking to Miss French.

MYERS. You were sure it was the prisoner you heard?

JANET. Aye, I know his voice well enough. With him calling so often. An agreeable voice it was, I'll not say it wasn't. Talking and laughing they were. But it was no business of mine so I went up and fetched the pattern, came down and let myself out and went back to my friend.

MYERS. Now I want these times very exact. You say that you re-entered the house at twenty-five past nine.

JANE. Aye. It was just after twenty past nine when I left Glenister Road.

MYERS. How do you know that, Miss MacKenzie?

JANET. By the clock on my friend's mantelpiece, and I compared it with my watch and the time was the same.

MYERS. You say it takes three or four minutes to walk to the house, so that you entered the house at twenty-five minutes past nine, and you were there . . .

JANET. I was there under ten minutes. It took me a few minutes to search for the pattern as I wasna' sure where I'd left it.

MYERS. And what did you do next?

JANET. I went back to my friend in Glenister Road. She was delighted with the pattern, simply delighted. I stayed there until twenty to eleven, then I said good night to them and came home. I went into the sitting-room then to see if the mistress wanted anything before she went to bed.

MYERS. What did you see?

JANET. She was there on the floor, poor body, her head beaten in. And all the drawers of the bureau out on the ground, everything tossed hither and thither, the broken vase on the floor and the curtains flying in the wind.

MYERS. What did you do?

JANET. I rang the police.

MYERS. Did you really think that a burglary had occurred?

SIR WILFRID. *(Jumping up)* Really, my lord, I must protest. *(He sits.)*

JUDGE. I will not allow that question to be answered, Mr. Myers. It should not have been put to the witness.

MYERS. Then let me ask you this, Miss MacKenzie. What did you do after you had telephoned the police?

JANET. I searched the house.

MYERS. What for?

JANET. For an intruder.

MYERS. Did you find one?

JANET. I did not. Nor any signs of disturbance save in the sitting-room.

MYERS. How much did you know about the prisoner, Leonard Vole?

JANET. I knew that he needed money.

MYERS. Did he ask Miss French for money?

JANET. He was too clever for that.

MYERS. Did he help Miss French with her business affairs—with her income tax returns, for instance?

JANET. Aye—not that there was any need of it.

MYERS. What do you mean by not any need of it?

JANET. Miss French had a good, clear head for business.

MYERS. Were you aware of what arrangements Miss French had made for the disposal of her money in the event of her death?

JANET. She'd make a will as the fancy took her. She was a rich woman and she had a lot of money to leave and no near relatives. "It must go where it can do the most good," she would say. Once it was to orphans she left it, and once to an old people's home, and another time a dispensary for cats and dogs, but it always came to the same in the end. She'd quarrel with the people and then she'd come home and tear up the will and make a new one.

MYERS. Do you know when she made her last will?

JANET. She made it on October the eigthth. I heard her speaking to Mr. Stokes, the lawyer. Saying he was to come tomorrow, she was making a new will. He was there at the time—the prisoner, I mean, kind of protesting, saying, "No, no."

(LEONARD *hastily scribbles a note.*)

And the mistress said, "But I want to, my dear boy. I want to. Remember that day I was nearly run over by a bus. It might happen any time."

(LEONARD *leans over the dock and hands the note to*
MAYHEW, *who passes it to* SIR WILFIRD.)

MYERS. Do you know when your mistress made a will previous to that one?

JANET. In the spring it was.

MYERS. Were you aware, Miss MacKenzie, that Leonard Vole was a married man?

JANET. No, indeed. Neither was the mistress.

SIR WILFRID. *(Rising)* I object. What Miss French knew or did not know is pure conjecture on Janet Mac-Kenzie's part. *(He sits.)*

MYERS. Let us put it this way: You formed the opinion that Miss French thought Leonard Vole a single man? Have you any facts to support that opinion?

JANET. There was the books she ordered from the library. There was the *Life of Baroness Burdett Coutts* and one about Disraeli and his wife. Both of them about women who'd married men years younger than themselves. I knew what she was thinking.

JUDGE. I'm afraid we cannot admit that.

JANET. Why?

JUDGE. Members of the Jury, it is possible for a woman to read the life of Disraeli without contemplating marriage with a man younger than herself.

MYERS. Did Mr. Vole ever mention a wife?

JANET. Never.

MYERS. Thank you. *(He sits.)*

SIR WILFRID. *(Rises. Gently and kindly.)* I think we all appreciate how very devoted to your mistress you were.

JANET. Aye—I was.

SIR WILFRID. You had great influence over her?

JANET. Aye—maybe.

SIR WILFRID. In the last will Miss French made—that is to say the one made last spring, Miss French left almost the whole of her fortune to you. Were you aware of that fact?

JANET. She told me so. "All crooks, these charities," she said. "Expenses here and expenses there and the money not going to the object you give it for. I've left it to you, Janet, and you can do what you think's right and good with it."

SIR WILFRID. That was an expression of great trust on her part. In her present will, I understand, she has merely left you an annuity. The principal beneficiary is the prisoner, Leonard Vole.

JANET. It will be wicked injustice if he ever touches a penny of that money.

SIR WILFRID. Miss French, you say, had not many friends and acquaintances. Now why was that?

JANET. She didn't go out much.

SIR WILFRID. When Miss French struck up this friendship with Leonard Vole it made you very sore and angry, didn't it?

JANET. I didn't like seeing my dear lady imposed upon.

SIR WILFRID. But you have admitted that Mr. Vole did not impose upon her. Perhaps you mean that you didn't like to see someone else supplanting you as an influence on Miss French?

JANET. She leaned on him a good deal. Far more than was safe, I thought.

SIR WILFRID. Far more than you personally liked?

JANET. Of course. I've said so. But it was of her good I was thinking.

SIR WILFRID. So the prisoner had a great influence over Miss French, and she had a great affection for him?

JANET. That was what it had come to.

SIR WILFRID. So that if the prisoner had ever asked her for money, she would almost certainly have given him some, would she not?

JANET. I have not said that.

SIR WILFRID. But he never received any money from her?

JANET. That may not have been for want of trying.

SIR WILFRID. Returning to the night of October the fourteenth, you say you heard the prisoner and Miss French talking together. What did you hear them say?

JANET. I didn't hear what they actually said.

SIR WILFRID. You mean you only heard the voices— the murmur of voices?

JANET. They were laughing.

SIR WILFRID. You heard a man's voice and a woman's and they were laughing. Is that right?

JANET. Aye.

SIR WILFRID. I suggest that is exactly what you did hear. A man's voice and a woman's voice laughing. You didn't hear what was said. What makes you say that the man's voice was Leonard Vole's?

JANET. I know his voice well enough.

SIR WILFRID. The door was closed, was it not?

JANET. Aye. It was closed.

SIR WILFRID. You heard a murmur of voices through a closed door and you swear that one of the voices was that of Leonard Vole. I suggest that that is mere prejudice on your part.

JANET. It was Leonard Vole.

SIR WILFRID. As I understand it you passed the door twice, once going to your room, and once going out?

JANET. That is so.

SIR WILFRID. You were no doubt in a hurry to get your pattern and return to your friend?

JANET. I was in no particular hurry. I had the whole evening.

SIR WILFRID. What I am suggesting is that on both occasions you walked quickly past that door.

JANET. I was there long enough to hear what I heard.

SIR WILFRID. Come, Miss MacKenzie, I'm sure you don't wish to suggest to the Jury that you were eavesdropping.

JANET. I was doing no such thing. I've better things to do with my time.

SIR WILFRID. Exactly. You are registered, of course, under the National Health Insurance?

JANET. That's so. Four and sixpence I have to pay out every week. It's a terrible lot of money for a working woman to pay.

SIR WILFRID. Yes, yes, many people feel that. I think, Miss MacKenzie, that you recently applied for a national hearing apparatus?

JANET. Six months ago I applied for it and not got it yet.

SIR WILFRID. So your hearing isn't very good, is that right? *(He lowers his voice.)* When I say to you, Miss MacKenzie, that you could not possibly recognize a voice through a closed door, what do you answer? *(He pauses.)* Can you tell me what I said?

JANET. I can no' hear anyone if they mumble.

SIR WILFRID. In fact you didn't hear what I said, although I am only a few feet from you in an open court. Yet you say that behind a closed door with two people talking in an ordinary conversational tone, you definitely recognized the voice of Leonard Vole as you swept past that door on two occasions.

JANET. It was him, I tell you. It was him.

SIR WILFRID. What you mean is you want it to be him. You have a preconceived notion.

JANET. Who else could it have been?

SIR WILFRID. Exactly. Who else could it have been? That was the way your mind worked. Now tell me, Miss MacKenzie, was Miss French sometimes lonely all by herself in the evening?

JANET. No, she was not lonely. She had books from the library.

SIR WILFRID. She listened to the wireless, perhaps?

JANET. Aye, she listened to the wireless.

SIR WILFRID. She was fond of a talk on it, perhaps, or of a good play?

JANET. Yes, she liked a good play.

SIR WILFRID. Wasn't it possible that on that evening when you returned home and passed the door, that what you really heard was the wireless switched on and a man and woman's voice, and laughter? There was a play called *Lover's Leap* on the wireless that night.

JANET. It was not the wireless.

SIR WILFRID. Oh, why not?

JANET. The wireless was away being repaired that week.

SIR WILFRID. *(Slightly taken aback.)* It must have upset you very much, Miss MacKenzie, if you really thought Miss French intended to marry the prisoner.

JANET. Naturally it would upset me. It was a *daft* thing to do.

SIR WILFRID. For one thing, *if* Miss French had married the prisoner it's quite possible, isn't it, that he might have persuaded her to dismiss you.

JANET. She'd never have done that, after all these years.

SIR WILFRID. But you never know what anyone will do, do you? Not if they're strongly influenced by anyone.

JANET. He would have used his influence, oh yes, he would have done his best to make her get rid of me.

SIR WILFRID. I see. You felt the prisoner was a very real menace to your present way of life at the time.

JANET. He'd have changed everything.

SIR WILFRID. Yes, very upsetting. No wonder you feel so bitterly against the prisoner. *(He sits.)*

MYERS. *(Rising)* My learned friend has been at great pains to extract from you an admission of vindictiveness towards the prisoner . . .

SIR WILFRID. *(Without rising, and audibly for the benefit of the Jury)* A painless extraction—quite painless.

MYERS. *(Ignoring him)* Did you really believe your mistress might have married the prisoner?

JANET. Indeed I did. I've just said so.

MYERS. Yes, indeed you have. In your view had the prisoner such an influence over Miss French that he could have persuaded her to dismiss you?

JANET. I'd like to have seen him try. He'd not have succeeded.

MYERS. Had the prisoner ever shown any dislike of you in any way?

JANET. No, he had his manners.

MYERS. Just one more question. You say you recognized Leonard Vole's voice through that closed door. Will you tell the Jury how you knew it was his?

JANET. You know a person's voice without hearing exactly what they are saying.

MYERS. Thank you, Miss MacKenzie.

JANET. *(To the* JUDGE.*)* Good morning. *(She stands down and crosses to the door up* L.*)*

MYERS. Call Thomas Clegg.

(The POLICEMAN *opens the door.)*

USHER. *(Rising and crossing to* C.*)* Thomas Clegg.
POLICEMAN. *(Calling)* Thomas Clegg.

*(*JANET *exits.* THOMAS CLEGG *enters up* L. *He carries a notebook. The* POLICEMAN *closes the door. The* USHER *moves to the witness box and picks up the Bible and oath card.* CLEGG *crosses and enters the witness box and takes the Bible from the* USHER.*)*

CLEGG. *(Saying the oath by heart)* I swear by Almighty God that the evidence that I shall give shall be the truth, the whole truth and nothing but the truth. *(He puts the Bible on the ledge of the witness box.)*

(The USHER puts the oath card on the ledge of the witness box, crosses and resumes his seat.)

MYERS. You are Thomas Clegg?
CLEGG. Yes, sir.
MYERS. You are an assistant in the forensic laboratory at New Scotland Yard?
CLEGG. I am.
MYERS. *(Indicating the jacket on the table)* Do you recognize that coat?

(The USHER rises, crosses to the table and picks up the jacket.)

CLEGG. Yes. It was given to me by Inspector Hearne and tested by me for traces of blood.

(The USHER hands the coat up to CLEGG, who brushes it aside. The USHER replaces the jacket on the table, crosses and resumes his seat.)

MYERS. Will you tell me your findings?
CLEGG. The coat sleeves had been washed, though not properly pressed afterwards, but by certain tests I am able to state that there are traces of blood on the cuffs.
MYERS. Is this blood of a special group or type?
CLEGG. Yes. *(He refers to his notebook.)* It is of the type O.
MYERS. Were you also given a sample of blood to test?
CLEGG. I was given a sample labelled "Blood of Miss Emily French." The blood group was of the same type —O.

(MYERS resumes his seat.)

SIR WILFRID. *(Rising)* You say there were traces of blood on both cuffs?

CLEGG. That is right.

SIR WILFRID. I suggest that there were traces of blood on only one cuff—the left one.

CLEGG. *(Looking at his notebook)* Yes. I am sorry, I made a mistake. It was only the left cuff.

SIR WILFRID. And it was only the left sleeve that had been washed?

CLEGG. Yes, that is so.

SIR WILFRID. Are you aware that the prisoner had told the police that he had cut his wrist, and that that blood was on the cuff of this coat?

CLEGG. So I understand.

(SIR WILFRID *takes a certificate from his* ASSISTANT.)

SIR WILFRID. I have here a certificate stating that Leonard Vole is a blood donor at the North London Hospital, and that is blood group is O. That is the same blood group, is it not?

CLEGG. Yes.

SIR WILFRID. So the blood might equally well have come from a cut on the prisoner's wrist?

CLEGG. That is so.

(SIR WILFRID *resumes his seat.)*

MYERS. *(Rising)* Blood group O is a very common one, is it not?

CLEGG. O? Oh, yes. At least forty-two per cent of people are in blood group O.

MYERS. Call Romaine Heilger.

(CLEGG *stands down and crosses to the door up* L.)

USHER. *(Rising and crossing to* C.) Romaine Heilger.

POLICEMAN. *(Opens the door. Calling)* Romaine Heilger.

(CLEGG exits. ROMAINE enters up L. There is a general buzz of conversation in the Court as she crosses to the witness box. The POLICEMAN closes the door. The USHER moves to the witness box and picks up the Bible and oath card.)

USHER. Silence! *(He hands the Bible to ROMAINE and holds up the card.)*

ROMAINE. I swear by Almighty God that the evidence that I shall give shall be the truth, the whole truth and nothing but the truth.

(The USHER replaces the Bible and oath card on the ledge of the witness box, crosses and resumes his seat.)

MYERS. Your name is Romaine Heilger?

ROMAINE. Yes.

MYERS. You have been living as the wife of the prisoner, Leonard Vole?

ROMAINE. Yes.

MYERS. Are you actually his wife?

ROMAINE. I went through a form of marriage with him in Berlin. My former husband is still alive, so the marriage is not . . . *(She breaks off.)*

MYERS. Not valid.

SIR WILFRID. *(Rising)* My lord, I have the most serious objection to this witness giving evidence at all. We have the undeniable fact of marriage between this witness and the prisoner, and no proof whatsoever of this so-called previous marriage.

MYERS. If my friend had not abandoned his customary patience, and had waited for one more question, your lordship would have been spared this further interruption.

(SIR WILFRID resumes his seat.)

(He picks up a document.) Mrs. Heilger, is this a cer-certificate of a marriage between yourself and Otto Gerthe Heilger on the eighteenth of April, nineteen forty-six, in Leipzig?

(The USHER *rises, takes the certificate from* MYERS *and takes it to* ROMAINE.)

ROMAINE. It is.

JUDGE. I should like to see that certificate.

(The USHER *gives the certificate to the* CLERK, *who hands it to the* JUDGE.)

It will be exhibit number four, I think.

MYERS. I believe it will be, my lord.

JUDGE. *(After examining the document.)* I think, Sir Wilfrid, this witness is competent to give evidence. *(He hands the certificate to the* CLERK.)

(The CLERK *gives the certificate to the* USHER, *who hands it to* MAYHEW. *The* USHER *then crosses and resumes his seat.* MAYHEW *shows the certificate to* SIR WILFRID.)

MYERS. In any event, Mrs. Heilger, are you willing to give evidence against the man you have been calling your husband?

ROMAINE. I'm quite willing.

(LEONARD *rises, followed by the* WARDER.)

LEONARD. Romaine! What are you doing here?—what are you saying?

JUDGE. I must have silence. As your counsel will tell you, Vole, you will very shortly have an opportunity of speaking in your own defence.

(LEONARD *and the* WARDER *resume their seats.)*

MYERS. *(To* ROMAINE.) Will you tell me in your own words what happened on the evening of October the fourteenth.

ROMAINE. I was at home all the evening.

MYERS. And Leonard Vole?

ROMAINE. Leonard went out at half past seven.

MYERS. When did he return?

ROMAINE. At ten minutes past ten.

(LEONARD *rises, followed by the* WARDER.)

LEONARD. That's not true. You know it's not true. It was about twenty-five past nine when I came home.
(MAYHEW *rises, turns to* LEONARD *and whispers to him to be quiet.*)
Who's been making you say this? I don't understand. *(He shrinks back and puts his hands to his face. Half whispering.)* I—I don't understand. *(He resumes his seat.)*

(MAYHEW *and the* WARDER *sit.*)

MYERS. Leonard Vole returned, you say, at ten minutes past ten? And what happened next?

ROMAINE. He was breathing hard, very excited. He threw off his coat and examined the sleeves. Then he told me to wash the cuffs. They had blood on them.

MYERS. Did he speak about the blood?

ROMAINE. He said, "Dammit, there's blood on them."

MYERS. What did you say?

ROMAINE. I said, "What have you done?"

MYERS. What did the prisoner say to that?

ROMAINE. He said, "I've killed her."

LEONARD. *(Rising; frenzied.)* It's not true, I tell you. It's not true.

(*The* WARDER *rises and restrains* LEONARD.)

JUDGE. Please control yourself.

LEONARD. Not a word of this is true. *(He resumes his seat.)*

(*The* WARDER *remains standing.*)

JUDGE. *(To* ROMAINE.) You know what you're saying, Mrs. Heilger?

ROMAINE. I am to speak the truth, am I not?

MYERS. The prisoner said, "I have killed her." Did you know to whom he referred?

ROMAINE. Yes, I knew. It was the old woman he had been going to see so often.

MYERS. What happened next?

ROMAINE. He told me that I was to say he had been at home with me all that evening, especially he said I was to say he was at home at half past nine. I said to him, "Do the police know you've killed her?" And he said, "No, they will think it's a burglary. But anyway, remember I was at home with you at half past nine."

MYERS. And you were subsequently interrogated by the police?

ROMAINE. Yes.

MYERS. Did they ask you if Leonard Vole was at home with you at half past nine?

ROMAINE. Yes.

MYERS. What did you answer to that?

ROMAINE. I said that he was.

MYERS. But you have changed your story now. Why?

ROMAINE. *(With sudden passion.)* Because it is murder. I cannot go on lying to save him. I am grateful to him, yes. He married me and brought me to this country. What he has asked me to do always I have done it because I was grateful.

MYERS. Because you loved him?

ROMAINE. No, I never loved him.

LEONARD. Romaine!

ROMAINE. I never loved him.

MYERS. You were grateful to the prisoner. He brought you to this country. He asked you to give him an alibi and at first you consented, but later you felt that what he had asked you to do was wrong?

ROMAINE. Yes, that is it exactly.

MYERS. Why did you feel it was wrong?

ROMAINE. When it is murder. I cannot come into Court and lie and say that he was there with me at the time it was done. I cannot do it. I cannot *do* it.

MYERS. So what did you do?

ROMAINE. I did not know what to do. I do not know your country and I am afraid of the police. So I write a letter to my ambassador, and I say that I do not wish to tell any more lies. I wish to speak the truth.

MYERS. That *is* the truth—that Leonard Vole returned that night at ten minutes past ten. That he had blood on the sleeves of his coat, that he said to you, "I have killed her." That is the truth before God?

ROMAINE. That is the truth.

(MYERS *resumes his seat.*)

SIR WILFRID. *(Rising)* When the prisoner went through this form of marriage with you, was he aware that your first husband was still alive?

ROMAINE. No.

SIR WILFRID. He acted in good faith?

ROMAINE. Yes.

SIR WILFRID. And you were very grateful to him?

ROMAINE. I was grateful to him, yes.

SIR WILFRID. You've shown your gratitude by coming here and testifying against him.

ROMAINE. I have to speak the truth.

SIR WILFRID. *(Savagely.)* Is it the truth?

ROMAINE. Yes.

SIR WILFRID. I suggest to you that on the night of October the fourteenth Leonard Vole was at home with you at nine-thirty, the time that the murder was committed. I suggest to you that this whole story of yours is a wicked fabrication, that you have for some reason a grudge against the prisoner, and that this is your way of expressing it.

ROMAINE. No.

SIR WILFRID. You realize that you are on oath?

ROMAINE. Yes.

SIR WILFRID. I warn you, Mrs. Heilger, that if you care nothing for the prisoner, be careful on your own account. The penalty for perjury is heavy.

MYERS. *(Rising and interposing)* Really, my lord. I don't know whether these theatrical outbursts are for the benefit of the Jury, but I do most respectfully submit that there is nothing to suggest that this witness has spoken anything but the truth.

JUDGE. Mr. Myers. This is a capital charge, and within the bounds of reason I would like the defence to have every lattitude. Yes, Sir Wilfrid.

(MYERS *resumes his seat.*)

SIR WILFRID. Now then. You have said—that there was blood on both cuffs?

ROMAINE. Yes.

SIR WILFRID. *Both* cuffs?

ROMAINE. I have told you, that is what Leonard said.

SIR WILFRID. No, Mrs. Heilger, you said, "He told me to wash the cuffs. They had blood on them."

JUDGE. That is precisely my note, Sir Wilfrid.

SIR WILFRID. Thank you, my lord. *(To* ROMAINE.) What you were saying is that you had washed both cuffs.

MYERS. *(Rising)* It is my friend's turn to be inaccurate now, my lord. Nowhere has this witness said she washed both cuffs, or indeed that she washed even one. *(He sits.)*

SIR WILFRID. My friend is right. Well, Mrs. Heilger, did you wash the sleeves?

ROMAINE. I remember now. It was only one sleeve that I washed.

SIR WILFRID. Thank you. Perhaps your memory as to other parts of your story is equally untrustworthy. I think your original story to the police was that the blood on the jacket came from a cut caused while carving ham?

ROMAINE. I said so, yes. But it was not true.

SIR WILFRID. Why did you lie?

ROMAINE. I said what Leonard told me to say.

SIR WILFRID. Even going so far as to produce the actual knife with which he was cutting the ham?

ROMAINE. When Leonard found he had blood on him, he cut himself to make it seem the blood was his.

LEONARD. *(Rising)* I never did.

SIR WILFRID. *(Silencing* LEONARD) Please, please.

(LEONARD *resumes his seat.)*

(To ROMAINE.) So you admit that your original story to the police was all lies? You seem to be a very good liar.

ROMAINE. Leonard told me what to say.

SIR WILFRID. The question is whether you were lying then or whether you are lying *now.* If you were really appalled at murder having been committed, you could have told the truth to the police when they first questioned you.

ROMAINE. I was afraid of Leonard.

SIR WILFRID. *(Gesturing towards the woeful figure of* LEONARD) You were afraid of Leonard Vole—afraid of the man whose heart and spirit you've just broken. I think the Jury will know which of you to believe. *(He sits.)*

MYERS. *(Rising)* Romaine Heilger. I ask you once more, is the evidence you have given the truth, the whole truth and nothing but the truth?

ROMAINE. It is.

MYERS. My lord, that is the case for the prosecution. *(He sits.)*

(ROMAINE *stands down and crosses to the door up* L. *The* POLICEMAN *opens the door.)*

LEONARD. *(As* ROMAINE *passes him.)* Romaine!

USHER. *(Rising)* Silence!

(ROMAINE *exits up* L. *The* POLICEMAN *closes the door. The* USHER *resumes his seat.)*

JUDGE. Sir Wilfrid.

SIR WILFRID. *(Rising)* My lord, members of the Jury, I will not submit to you, as I might, that there is no case for the prisoner to answer. There *is* a case. A case of very strong circumstantial evidence. You have heard the police and other expert witnesses. They have given fair, impartial evidence as is their duty. Against them I have nothing to say. On the other hand, you have heard Janet MacKenzie and the woman who calls herself Romaine Vole. Can you believe that their testimony is not warped? Janet MacKenzie—cut out of her rich mistress's will because her position was usurped, quite unwittingly, by this unfortunate boy. *(He pauses.)* Romaine Vole—Heilger—whatever she calls herself, who trapped him into marriage, whilst concealing from him the fact that she was married already. That woman owes him more than she can ever repay. She used him to save her from political persecution. But she admits no love for him. He has served his purpose. I will ask you to be very careful how you believe her testimony, the testimony of a woman who, for all we know, has been brought up to believe the pernicious doctrine that lying is a weapon to be used to serve one's own ends. Members of the Jury, I call the prisoner. Leonard Vole.

(The USHER *rises and crosses to the witness box.* LEONARD *rises, crosses and goes into the witness box. The* WARDER *follows* LEONARD *and stands behind him. The* USHER *picks up the Bible, hands it to* LEONARD *and holds up the oath card.)*

LEONARD. I swear by Almighty God that the evidence that I shall give shall be the truth, the whole truth and nothing but the truth. *(He puts the Bible on the ledge of the witness box.)*

(The USHER *replaces the oath card on the ledge of the witness box and sits* R. *of the table.)*

SIR WILFRID. Now, Mr. Vole, we have heard of your friendship with Miss Emily French. Now I want you to tell us how often you visited her.

LEONARD. Frequently.

SIR WILFRID. Why was that?

LEONARD. Well, she was awfully nice to me and I got fond of her. She was like my Aunt Betsy.

SIR WILFRID. That was an aunt who brought you up?

LEONARD. Yes. She was a dear. Miss French reminded me of her.

SIR WILFRID. You've heard Janet MacKenzie say Miss French thought you were a single man, and that there was some question of marrying you. Is there any truth in this?

LEONARD. Of course. Not. It's an absurd idea.

SIR WILFRID. Miss French knew that you were married?

LEONARD. Yes.

SIR WILFRID. So there was no question of marriage between you?

LEONARD. Of course not. I've told you, she treated me as though she was an indulgent aunt. Almost like a mother.

SIR WILFRID. And in return you did everything for her that you could.

LEONARD. (Simply.) I was very fond of her.

SIR WILFRID. Will you tell the Jury in your own words exactly what happened on the night of October the fourteenth?

LEONARD. Well, I'd come across a kind of a cat brush —a new thing in that line—and I thought it would please her. So I took it along that evening. I'd nothing else to do.

SIR WILFRID. What time was that?

LEONARD. Just before eight I got there. I gave her the cat brush. She was pleased. We tried it out on one of the cats and it was a success. Then we played a game of Double Demon—Miss French was very fond of Double Demon—and after that I left.

SIR WILFRID. Yes, but did you not . . .

JUDGE. Sir Wilfrid, I don't understand this piece of evidence at all. What is a cat brush?

LEONARD. It's a brush for brushing cats.

JUDGE. Oh!

LEONARD. A sort of brush and comb combined. Miss French kept cats—eight of them she had, and the house smelt a bit . . .

SIR WILFRID. Yes, yes.

LEONARD. I thought the brush might be useful.

SIR WILFRID. Did you see Janet MacKenzie?

LEONARD. No. Miss French let me in herself.

SIR WILFRID. Did you know Janet MacKenzie was out?

LEONARD. Well, I didn't think about it.

SIR WILFRID. At what time did you leave?

LEONARD. Just before nine. I walked home.

SIR WILFORD. How long did that take you?

LEONARD. Oh, I should say about twenty minutes to half an hour.

SIR WILFRID. So that you reached home . . .?

LEONARD. I reached home at twenty-five minutes past nine.

SIR WILFRID. And your wife—I will call her your wife —was at home then?

LEONARD. Yes, of course she was. I—I think she must have gone mad. I . . .

SIR WILFRID. Never mind that now. Just go on with your story. Did you wash your coat when you got in?

LEONARD. No, of course I didn't.

SIR WILFRID. Who did wash your coat?

LEONARD. Romaine did, the next morning. She said it had got blood on it from a cut on my wrist.

SIR WILFRID. A cut on your wrist?

LEONARD. Yes. Here. *(He holds out his arm and shows his wrist.)* You can still see the mark.

SIR WILFRID. When was the first you heard of the murder?

LEONARD. I read about it in the evening paper the next day.

SIR WILFRID. And what did you feel?

LEONARD. I was stunned. I could hardly believe it. I was very upset too. The papers said it was a burglary. I never dreamed of anything else.

SIR WILFRID. And what happened next?

LEONARD. I read that the police were anxious to interview me, so of course I went along to the police station.

SIR WILFRID. You went along to the police station and made a statement?

LEONARD. Yes.

SIR WILFRID. You were not nervous? Reluctant to do so?

LEONARD. No, of course not. I wanted to help in any way possible.

SIR WILFRID. Did you ever receive any money from Miss French?

LEONARD. No.

SIR WILFRID. Were you aware that she had made a will in your favour?

LEONARD. She said she was ringing up her lawyers and going to make a new will. I asked her if she often made new wills and she said, "From time to time."

SIR WILFRID. Did you know what the terms of this new will were to be?

LEONARD. I swear I didn't.

SIR WILFRID. Had she ever suggested to you that she might leave you anytning at all in her will?

LEONARD. No.

SIR WILFRID. You have heard the evidence that your wife—or the woman whom you considered as your wife —has given in Court.

LEONARD. Yes—I heard. I can't understand—I . . .

SIR WILFRID. (Checking him) I realize, Mr. Vole, that you are very upset, but I want to ask you to put aside all emotion and to answer the question plainly and simply. Was what that witness said true or untrue?

LEONARD. No, of course it wasn't true.

SIR WILFRID. You arrived home at nine-twenty-five that night, and had supper with your wife?

LEONARD. Yes.

SIR WILFRID. Did you go out again?

LEONARD. No.

SIR WILFRID. Are you right or left handed?

LEONARD. Right handed.

SIR WILFRID. I'm going to ask you just one more question, Mr. Vole. *Did you kill* Emily French?

LEONARD. No, I did not.

(SIR WILFRID *sits.*)

MYERS. *(Rising)* Have you ever tried to get money out of anybody?

LEONARD. No.

MYERS. How soon in your acquaintance with Miss French did you learn that she was a very wealthy woman?

LEONARD. Well, I didn't know she *was* rich when I first went to see her.

MYERS. But, having gained that knowledge, you decided to cultivate her acquaintance further?

LEONARD. I suppose that's what it looks like. But I really liked her, you know. Money had nothing to do with it.

MYERS. You would have continued to visit her, no matter how poor she'd been?

LEONARD. Yes, I would.

MYERS. You yourself are in poor circumstances?

LEONARD. You know I am.

MYERS. Kindly answer the question, yes or no.

JUDGE. You must answer the question, yes or no.

LEONARD. Yes.

MYERS. What salary do you earn?

LEONARD. Well, as a matter of fact I haven't got a job at the moment. Haven't had one for some time.

MYERS. You were recently discharged from your position?

LEONARD. No, I wasn't—I quit.

MYERS. At the time of your arrest how much money had you in the bank?

LEONARD. Well, actually only a few pounds. I was expecting some money in, in a week or two.

MYERS. How much?

LEONARD. Not very much.

MYERS. I put it to you, you were pretty desperate for money?

LEONARD. Not desperate. I—well, I felt a bit worried.

MYERS. You were worried about money, you met a wealthy woman and you courted her acquaintance assiduously.

LEONARD. You make it sound all twisted. I tell you I liked her.

MYERS. We have heard that Miss French used to consult you on her income tax returns.

LEONARD. Yes, she did. You know what those forms are. You can't make head or tail of them—or she couldn't.

MYERS. Janet MacKenzie has told us that Miss French was a very good business woman, well able to deal with her own affairs.

LEONARD. Well, that's not what she said to me. She said those forms worried her terribly.

MYERS. In filling up her income tax forms for her you no doubt learned the exact amount of her income?

LEONARD. No.

MYERS. No?

LEONARD. Well—I mean naturally, yes.

MYERS. Yes, very convenient. How was it, Mr. Vole, that you never took your wife to see Miss French?

LEONARD. I don't know. It just didn't seem to crop up.

MYERS. You say Miss French knew you were married?

LEONARD. Yes.

MYERS. Yet she never asked you to bring your wife with you to the house?

LEONARD. No.

MYERS. Why not?

LEONARD. Oh, I don't know. She didn't like women, I don't think.

MYERS. She preferred, shall we say, personable young men? And you didn't insist on bringing your wife?

LEONARD. No, of course I didn't. You see, she knew my wife was a foreigner and she—oh, I don't know, she seemed to think we didn't get on.

MYERS. That was the impression you gave her?

LEONARD. No, I didn't. She—well, I think it was wishful thinking on her part.

MYERS. You mean she was infatuated with you?

LEONARD. No, she wasn't infatuated, but she, oh, it's like mothers are sometimes with a son.

MYERS. How?

LEONARD. They don't want him to like a girl or get engaged or anything of that kind.

MYERS. You hoped, didn't you, for some monetary advantage from your friendship with Miss French?

LEONARD. Not in the way you mean.

MYERS. Not in the way I mean? You seem to know what I mean better than I know myself. In what way then did you hope for monetary advantage? *(He pauses.)* I repeat, in what way did you hope for monetary advantage?

LEONARD. You see, there's a thing I've invented. A kind of windscreen wiper that works in snow. I was looking for someone to finance that and I thought perhaps Miss French would. But that wasn't the only reason I went to see her. I tell you I liked her.

MYERS. Yes, yes, we've heard that very often, haven't we—how much you liked her.

LEONARD. *(Sulkily.)* Well, it's true.

MYERS. I believe, Mr. Vole, that about a week before Miss French's death, you were making enquiries of a travel agency for particulars of foreign cruises.

LEONARD. Supposing I did—it isn't a crime, is it?

MYERS. Not at all. Many people go for cruises *when they can pay for it*. But you couldn't pay for it, could you, Mr. Vole?

LEONARD. I was hard up. I told you so.

MYERS. And yet you came into this particular travel agency—with a blonde—a strawberry blonde—I understand—and . . .

JUDGE. A strawberry blonde, Mr. Myers?

MYERS. A term for a lady with reddish fair hair, my lord.

JUDGE. I thought I knew all about blondes, but a strawberry blonde . . . Go on, Mr. Myers.

MYERS. *(To* LEONARD.) Well?

LEONARD. My wife isn't a blonde and it was only a bit of fun, anyway.

MYERS. You admit that you asked for particulars, not of cheap trips, but of the most expensive and luxurious cruises. How did you expect to pay for such a thing?

LEONARD. I didn't.

MYERS. I suggest that you knew that in a week's time you would have inherited a large sum of money from a trusting elderly lady.

LEONARD. I didn't know anything of the kind. I just was feeling fed up—and there were the posters in the window —palm trees and coconuts and blue seas, and I went in and asked. The clerk gave me a sort of supercilious look —I *was* a bit shabby—but it riled me. And so I put on a bit of an act— *(He suddenly grins as though enjoying remembrance of the scene.)* and began asking for the swankiest tours there were—all *de luxe* and a cabin on the boat deck.

MYERS. You really expect the Jury to believe that?

LEONARD. I don't expect anyone to believe anything. But that's the way it was. It was make-believe and childish if you like—but it was fun and I enjoyed it. *(He looks suddenly pathetic.)* I wasn't thinking of killing anybody or of inheriting money.

MYERS. So it was just a remarkable coincidence that Miss French should be killed, leaving you her heir, only a few days later.

LEONARD. I've told you—I didn't kill her.

MYERS. Your story is that on the night of the fourteenth, you left Miss French's house at four minutes to nine, that you walked home and you arrived there at twenty-five minutes past nine, and stayed there the rest of the evening.

LEONARD. Yes.

MYERS. You have heard the woman Romaine Heilger rebut that story in Court. You have heard her say that you came in not at *twenty-five minutes* past nine but at *ten minutes past ten.*

LEONARD. It's not true!

MYERS. That your clothes were bloodstained, that you definitely admitted to her that you had killed Miss French.

LEONARD. It's not true, I tell you. Not one word of it is true.

MYERS. Can you suggest any reason why this young woman, who has been passing as your wife, should deliberately give evidence she has given if it were not true?

LEONARD. No, I can't. That's the awful thing. There's no reason at all. I think she must have gone mad.

MYERS. You think she must have gone mad? She seemed extremely sane, and self-possessed. But insanity is the only reason you can suggest.

LEONARD. I don't understand it. Ah, God, what's happened—what's changed her?

MYERS. Very effective, I'm sure. But in this Court we deal with facts. And the fact is, Mr. Vole, that we have only your word for it that you left Emily French's house at the time you say you did, and that you arrived home at five and twenty minutes past nine, and that you did not go out again.

LEONARD. *(Wildly.)* Someone must have seen me—in the street—or going into the house.

MYERS. One would certainly think so—but the only person who did see you come home that night says it was at ten minutes past ten. And that person says that you had blood on your clothes.

LEONARD. I cut my wrist.

MYERS. A very easy thing to do in case any questions should arise.

LEONARD. *(Breaking down)* You twist everything. You twist everything I say. You make me sound like a different kind of person from what I am.

MYERS. You cut your wrist deliberately.

LEONARD. No, I didn't. I didn't do anything, but you make it all sound as though I did. I can hear it myself.

MYERS. You came home at ten past ten.

LEONARD. No, I didn't. You've *got* to believe me. You've got to *believe* me.

MYERS. You killed Emily French.

LEONARD. I didn't do it.

(*The LIGHTS fade quickly, leaving two spots on* LEONARD *and* MYERS. *These fade too as he finishes speaking and the Curtain falls.*)

I didn't kill her. I've never killed anybody. Oh God! It's a nightmare. It's some awful, evil dream.

CURTAIN

ACT THREE

Scene I

SCENE: *The Chambers of Sir Wilfrid Robarts, Q.C. The same evening.*

When the Curtain rises, the stage is empty and in darkness. The window curtains are open. GRETA *enters immediately and holds the door open.* MAYHEW *and* SIR WILFRID *enter.* MAYHEW *carries his brief-case.*

GRETA. Good evening, Sir Wilfrid. It's a nasty night, sir. (GRETA *exits, closing the door behind her.*)

SIR WILFRID. Damned fog! *(He switches on the wall-brackets by the switch below the door and crosses to the window.)*

MAYHEW. It's a beast of an evening. *(He removes his hat and overcoat and hangs them on the pegs up* L.)

SIR WILFRID. *(Closing the window curtains)* Is there no justice? We come out of a stuffy Court Room gasping for fresh air, and what do we find? *(He switches on the desk lamp.)* Fog!

MAYHEW. It's not as thick as the fog we're in over Mrs. Heilger's antics. *(He crosses to the desk and puts his case on the up* L. *corner.)*

SIR WILFRID. That damned woman. From the very first moment I clapped eyes on her, I scented trouble. I knew she was up to something. A thoroughly vindictive piece of goods and much too deep for that simple young fool in the dock. But what's *her* game, John? What's she up to? Tell me that. *(He crosses below the desk to* L.)

82

MAYHEW. Presumably, it would seem, to get young Leonard Vole convicted of murder.

SIR WILFRED. *(Crossing down* R.*)* But why? Look what he's done for her.

MAYHEW. He's probably done too much for her.

SIR WILFRID. *(Moving up* R. *of the desk)* And she despises him for it. That's likely enough. Ungrateful beasts, women. But why be vindictive? After all, if she was bored with him, all she had to do was walk out. *(He crosses above the dek to* L.*)* There doesn't seem to be any financial reason for her to remain with him.

GRETA. *(Enters and crosses to the desk. She carries a tray with two cups of tea.)* I've brought you your tea, Sir Wilfrid, and a cup for Mr. Mayhew, too. *(She puts one cup on each side of the desk.)*

SIR WILFRID. *(Sitting* L. *of the fireplace)* Tea? Strong drink is what we need.

GRETA. Oh, you know you like your tea really, sir. How did it go today?

SIR WILFRID. Badly.

(MAYHEW sits L. *of the desk.)*

GRETA. *(Crossing to* SIR WILFRID*)* Oh, no, sir. Oh, I do hope not. Because he didn't do it. I'm sure he didn't do it. *(She crosses to the door.)*

SIR WILFRID. You're still sure he didn't do it. *(He looks thoughtfully at her.)* Now why's that?

GRETA. *(Confidently.)* Because he's not the sort. He's *nice,* if you know what I mean—ever so nice. He'd never go coshing an old lady on the head. But you'll get him off, won't you, sir?

SIR WILFRID. I'll—get—him—off.

(GRETA exits.)

(He rises. Almost to himself.) God knows how. Only one woman on the jury—pity—evidently the women like him —can't think why—he's not particularly— *(He crosses to* R. *of the desk.)* good looking. Perhaps he's got something

that arouses the maternal instinct. Women want to mother him.

MAYHEW. Whereas Mrs. Heilger—is *not* the maternal type.

SIR WILFRID. *(Picking up his tea and crossing with it to* L.) No, she's the passionate sort. Hot blooded behind that cool self-control. The kind that would knife a man if he double-crossed her. God, how I'd like to break her down. Show up her lies. Show *her* up for what she is.

MAYHEW. *(Rising and taking his pipe from his pocket)* Forgive me, Wilfrid, but aren't you letting this case become a personal duel between you and her? *(He moves to the fireplace, takes a pipe cleaner from the jar on the mantelpiece and cleans his pipe.)*

SIR WILFRID. Am I? Perhaps I am. But she's an evil woman, John. I'm convinced of that. And a young man's life depends on the outcome of that duel.

MAYHEW. *(Thoughtfully.)* I don't think the Jury liked her.

SIR WILFRID. No, you're right there, John. I don't think they did. To begin with, she's a foreigner, and they distrust foreigners. Then she's not married to the fellow—she's more or less admitting to committing bigamy.

(MAYHEW *tosses the pipe cleaner into the fireplace, then crosses to* L. *of the desk.)*

None of that goes down well. And at the end of it all, she's not sticking to her man when he's down. We don't like that in this country.

MAYHEW. That's all to the good.

SIR WILFRID. *(Crossing above the desk to* R. *of it)* Yes, but it isn't enough. There's no corroboration of his statements whatsoever. *(He puts his tea on the desk.)*

(MAYHEW *crosses to* L.)

He admits being with Miss French that evening, his fingerprints are all over the place, we haven't managed to find anybody who saw him on the way home, and there's the altogether damning matter of the will. *(He stands above the desk.)* That travel-agency business doesn't help. The woman makes a will in his favour and immediately he goes enquiring about luxury cruises. Couldn't be more unfortunate.

MAYHEW. *(Moving to the fireplace)* I agree. And his explanation was hardly convincing.

SIR WILFRID. *(With a sudden complete change of manner and becoming very human)* And yet, you know, John, my wife does it.

MAYHEW. Does what?

SIR WILFRID. *(Smiling indulgently.)* Gets travel agencies to make out itineraries for extensive foreign tours. For both of us. *(He takes the tobacco jar from the mantelpiece and puts it on the desk.)*

MAYHEW. Thank you, Wilfrid. *(He sits L. of the desk and fills his pipe.)*

SIR WILFRID. She'll work it all out to the last detail and bemoan the fact that the boat misses a connection at Bermuda. *(He moves to R. of the desk.)* She'll say to me that we could save time by flying but that we wouldn't see anything of the country, and— *(He sits R. of the desk.)* what do I think? And I say: "It's all the same to me, my dear. Arrange it as you like." We both know that it's a kind of game, and we'll end up with the same old thing—staying at home.

MAYHEW. Ah, now with *my* wife, it's houses.

SIR WILFRID. Houses?

MAYHEW. Orders to view. Sometimes I think that there's hardly a house in England that's ever been up for sale that my wife hasn't been over. She plans how to apportion the rooms, and works out any structural alterations that will be necessary. She even plans the curtains and the covers and the general colour scheme. *(He rises, puts the tobacco jar on the mantelpiece and feels in his pocket for match.)*

(SIR WILFRID *and* MAYHEW *look at each other and smile indulgently.)*

SIR WILFRID. H'm—well . . . *(He becomes the* Q.C.

again.) The fantasies of our wives aren't evidence, worse luck. But it helps one to understand why young Vole went asking for cruise literature.

MAYHEW. Pipe dreams.

SIR WILFRID. *(Taking a matchbox from the desk drawer)* There you are, John. *(He puts the box on the desk.)*

MAYHEW. *(Crossing to* L. *of the desk and picking up the matchbox)* Thank you, Wilfrid.

SIR WILFRID. I think we've had a certain amount of luck with Janet MacKenzie.

MAYHEW. Bias, you mean?

SIR WILFRID. That's right. Overdoing her prejudice.

MAYHEW. *(Sitting* L. *of the desk)* That was a very telling point of yours about her deafness.

SIR WILFRID. Yes, yes, we got her there. But she got her own back over the wireless.

(MAYHEW *finds that the matchbox is empty, throws it in the waste-paper basket and puts his pipe in his pocket.)*

Not smoking, John?

MAYHEW. No, not just now.

SIR WILFRID. John, what really happened that night? Was it robbery with violence after all? The police have to admit that it might have been.

MAYHEW. But they don't really think so and they don't often make a mistake. That inspector is quite convinced that it *was* an inside job—that that window was tampered with from the inside.

SIR WILFRID. *(Rising and crossing below the desk to* L.) Well, he may be wrong.

MAYHEW. I wonder.

SIR WILFRID. But if so who was the man Janet MacKenzie heard talking to Miss French at nine-thirty? Seems to me there are two answers to that.

MAYHEW. The answers being . . .?

SIR WILFRID. First that she made the whole thing up, when she saw that the police weren't satisfied about its being a burglary.

MAYHEW. *(Shocked.)* Surely she wouldn't do a thing like that?

SIR WILFRID. *(Crossing to* C.*)* Well, what did she hear, then? Don't tell me it was a burglar chatting amicably with Miss French— *(He takes his handkerchief from his pocket.)* before he coshed her on the head, you old clown. *(He coshes* MAYHEW *with the handkerchief.)*

MAYHEW. That certainly seems unlikely.

SIR WILFRID. I don't think that that rather grim old woman would stick at making up a thing like that. I don't think she'd stick at anything, you know. No— *(Significantly.)* I don't think—she'd stick—at—*anything*.

MAYHEW. *(Horrified.)* Good Lord! Do you mean . . .?

CARTER. *(Enters and closes the door behind him.)* Excuse me, Sir Wilfrid. A young woman is asking to see you. She says it has to do with the case of Leonard Vole.

SIR WILFRID. *(Unimpressed.)* Mental?

CARTER. Oh, no, Sir Wilfrid. I can always recognize that type.

SIR WILFRID. *(Moving above the desk and picking up the tea-cups)* What sort of a young woman? *(He crosses to* C.*)*

CARTER. *(Taking the cups from* SIR WILFRID*)* Rather a common young woman, sir, with a free way of talking.

SIR WILFRID. And what does she want?

CARTER. *(Quoting somewhat distastefully)* She says she "knows something that might do the prisoner a bit of good."

SIR WILFRID. *(With a sigh.)* Highly unlikely. Bring her in.

(CARTER *exits, taking the cups with him.)*

What do you think, John?

MAYHEW. Oh well, we can't afford to leave any stone unturned.

(CARTER *enters and ushers in a* WOMAN. *She appears to be aged almost thirty-five and is flamboyantly but cheaply dressed. Blonde hair falls over one side of her face. She is violently and crudely made up. She carries a shabby handbag.* MAYHEW *rises.)*

CARTER. The young lady. (CARTER *exits.*)

WOMAN. *(Looking sharply from* SIR WILFRID *to* MAYHEW) Here, what's this? Two o' yer? I'm not talking to two of yer. *(She turns to go.)*

SIR WILFRID. This is Mr. Mayhew. He is Leonard Vole's solicitor. I am Sir Wilfrid Robarts, Counsel for the Defence.

WOMAN. *(Peering at* SIR WILFRID) So you are, dear. Didn't recognize you without your wig. Lovely you all look in them wigs.

(MAYHEW *gives* SIR WILFRID *a nudge, then stands above the desk.)*

Havin' a bit of a confab, are you? Well, maybe I can help you if you make it worth my while.

SIR WILFRID. You know, Miss—er . . .

WOMAN. *(Crossing and sitting* L. *of the desk)* No need for names. If I did give you a name, it mightn't be the right one, might it?

SIR WILFRID. *(Standing* C.) As you please. You realize you are in duty bound to come forward to give any evidence that may be in your possession.

WOMAN. Aw, come off it! I didn't say I knew anything, did I? I've *got* something. That's more to the point.

MAYHEW. What is it you have got, madam?

WOMAN. Aye-aye! I was in court today. I watched that —that trollop give her evidence. So high and mighty about it too. She's a wicked one. A Jezebel, that's what she is.

SIR WILFRID. Quite so. But as to this special information you have . . .

WOMAN. *(Cunningly.)* Ah, but what's in it for me? It's valuable, what I've got. A hundred quid, that's what I want.

MAYHEW. I'm afraid we could not countenance anything of that character, but perhaps if you tell us a little more about what you have to offer . . .

WOMAN. You don't buy unless you get a butcher's, is that it?

SIR WILFRID. A butcher's?

WOMAN. A butcher's 'ook—look.

SIR WILFRID. Oh, yes—yes.

WOMAN. I've got the goods on her all right. *(She opens her handbag.)* It's letters, that's what it is. Letters.

SIR WILFRID. Letters written by Romaine Vole to the prisoner?

WOMAN. *(Laughing coarsely)* To the prisoner? Don't make me laugh. Poor ruddy prisoner, he's been took in by her all right. *(She winks.)* I've got something to *sell*, dear, and don't you forget it.

MAYHEW. *(Smoothly.)* If you will let us see these letters, we shall be able to advise you as to how pertinent they are.

WOMAN. Putting it in your own language, aren't you? Well, as I say, I don't expect you to buy without seeing. But fair's fair. If those letters will do the trick, if they'll get the boy off, and put that foreign bitch where she belongs, well, it's a hundred quid for me. Right?

MAYHEW. *(Taking his wallet from his pocket and extracting ten pounds)* If these letters contain information that is useful to the defence—to help your expenses in coming here—I am prepared to offer you ten pounds.

WOMAN. *(Almost screaming.)* Ten bloody quid for letters like these. Think again.

SIR WILFRID. *(Crossing to MAYHEW and taking the wallet from him)* If you have a letter there that will help to prove my client's innocence, twenty pounds would I think not be an unreasonable sum for your expenses. *(He crosses to R. of the desk, takes ten pounds from the wallet, returns the empty wallet to MAYHEW, and takes the first ten pounds from him.)*

WOMAN. Fifty quid and it's a bargain. That's if you're satisfied with the letters.

SIR WILFRID. Twenty pounds. *(He puts the notes on the desk.)*

(The WOMAN watches him and wets her lips. It is too much for her.)

WOMAN. All right, blast you. 'Ere, take 'em. Quite a packet of 'em. *(She takes the letters from her handbag.)* The top one's the one will do the trick. *(She puts the letters on the desk, then goes to pick up the money.)*

(SIR WILFRID *is too quick for the* WOMAN *and picks up the money. The* WOMAN *quickly retrieves the letters.)*

SIR WILFRID. Just a moment. I suppose this is her handwriting?

WOMAN. It's her handwriting all right. She wrote 'em. It's all fair and square.

SIR WILFRID. We have only your word for that.

MAYHEW. Just a moment. I have a letter from Mrs. Vole—not here, but at my office.

SIR WILFRID. Well, madam, it looks as though we'll have to trust you— *(He hands her the notes.)* for the moment. *(He takes the letters from her, smoothes them out and begins to read.)*

> *(The* WOMAN *slowly counts the notes, carefully watching the* OTHERS *meanwhile.* MAYHEW *moves to* SIR WILFRID *and peers at the letters. The* WOMAN *rises and crosses towards the door.)*

(To MAYHEW.) It's incredible. Quite incredible.

MAYHEW. *(Reading over his shoulder)* The cold-blooded vindictiveness.

SIR WILFRID. *(Crossing to the* WOMAN) How did you get hold of these?

WOMAN. That'd be telling.

SIR WILFRID. What have you got against Romaine Vole?

> *(The* WOMAN *crosses to the desk, suddenly and dramatically turns her head, swings the desk lamp so that it flows on to her face on the side that has been turned*

away from the audience, pushing her hair back as she does so, revealing that her cheek is all slashed, scarred and disfigured. SIR WILFRID starts back with an ejaculation.)

WOMAN. See that?

SIR WILFRID. Did *she* do that to you?

WOMAN. *(Crossing to C.)* Not her. The chap I was going with. Going with him steady, I was too. He was a bit younger than me, but he was fond of me and I loved him. Then she came along. She took a fancy to him and she got him away from me. She started to see him on the sly and then one day he cleared out. I knew where he'd gone. I went after him and I found them together. *(She sits L. of the desk.)* I told 'er what I thought of 'er and 'e set on me. In with one of the razor gangs, he was. He cut my face up proper. "There," he says, "no man'll ever look at you now."

SIR WILFRID. Did you go to the police about it?

WOMAN. Me? Not likely. 'Sides it wasn't 'is fault. Not really. It was hers, all hers. Getting him away from me, turning 'im against me. But I waited my time. I followed 'er about and watched 'er. I know some of the things she's bin up to. I know where the bloke lives who she goes to see on the sly sometimes. That's how I got hold of them letters. So now you know the whole story, mister. *(She rises, thrusts her face forward and pushes her hair aside.)* Want to kiss me?

(SIR WILFRID *shrinks back.*)

I don't blame yer. *(She crosses to L.)*

SIR WILFRID. I'm deeply sorry, deeply sorry. Got a fiver, John?

(MAYHEW *shows his empty wallet.*)

(He takes his wallet from his pocket and extracts a five-pound note.) Er—we'll make it another five pounds.

WOMAN. *(Grabbing the note)* 'Oldin' out on me, were yer? Willin' to go up another five quid. *(She advances on SIR WILFRID.)*

(SIR WILFRID *backs towards* MAYHEW.)

Ah, I knew I was being too soft with you. Those letters are the goods, aren't they?

SIR WILFRID. They will, I think, be very useful. *(He turns to* MAYHEW *and holds out a letter.)* Here, John, have a butcher's at this one.

(The WOMAN *slips quickly out of the door.)*

MAYHEW. We'll have a handwriting expert on these for safety's sake, and he can give evidence if necessary.

SIR WILFRID. We shall require this man's surname and his address.

MAYHEW. *(Looking around)* Hullo, where has she gone? She mustn't leave without giving us further particulars. *(He crosses to* C.*)*

SIR WILFRID. *(Crosses and exits hurriedly. Off, calling)* Carter! Carter!

CARTER. *(Off.)* Yes, Sir Wilfrid?

SIR WILFRID. *(Off.)* Carter, where did that young woman go?

CARTER. *(Off.)* She went straight out, sir.

SIR WILFRID. *(Off.)* Well, you shouldn't have let her go. Send Greta after her.

CARTER. *(Off.)* Very good, Sir Wilfrid.

*(*SIR WILFRID *enters and crosses to* L. *of* MAYHEW.*)*

MAYHEW. She's gone?

SIR WILFRID. Yes, I've sent Greta after her, but there's not a hope in this fog. Damn! We must have this man's surname and address.

MAYHEW. We won't get it. She thought things out too carefully. Wouldn't give us her name, and slipped out like an eel as soon as she saw us busy with the letters. She daren't risk having to appear in the witness box. Look what the man did to her last time.

SIR WILFRID. *(Without conviction)* She'd have protection.

MAYHEW. Would she? For how long? He'd get her in

the end, or his pals would. She's already risked something coming here. She doesn't want to bring the man into it. It's Romaine Heilger she's after.

SIR WILFRID. And what a beauty our Romaine is. But we've got something to go on at last. Now as to procedure . . .

CURTAIN

SCENE TWO

SCENE: *The Old Bailey. The next morning.*

When the Curtain rises, the Court is awaiting the entry of the JUDGE. LEONARD *and the* WARDER *are seated in the dock. Two* BARRISTERS *are seated at the* L. *end of the back row of* BARRISTERS' *seats.* SIR WILFRID *and his* ASSISTANT *are in their places.* MAYHEW *is standing* L. *of the table talking to* SIR WILFRID. *The* CLERK OF THE COURT, *the* JUDGE'S CLERK *and the* STENOGRAPHER *are in their places. The three visible* MEMBERS OF THE JURY *are seated. The* POLICEMAN *is at the doors up* L. *The* USHER *is standing at the top of the steps up* R.C. MYERS, *his* ASSISTANT *and two* BARRISTERS *enter up* C. MYERS *crosses to* SIR WILFRID *and starts talking angrily. The* ASSISTANT *and the* BARRISTERS *take their seats. There are three KNOCKS on the* JUDGE'S *door. The* USHER *comes down the steps to* R.C.

USHER. Stand up.
   (ALL *stand. The* JUDGE *and* ALDERMAN *enter by the* JUDGE'S *door and take their seats.)*
All persons who have anything further to do before my lady the Queen's justices of Oyer and Terminer and general gaol delivery for the jurisdiction of the Central Criminal Court draw near and give your attendance. God Save the Queen.

(The JUDGE bows to the Court and ALL take their seats. The USHER sits on the stool down R.)

SIR WILFRID. *(Rising)* My lord, since this was adjourned, certain evidence of a rather startling character has come into my hands. This evidence is such that I am taking it upon myself to ask your lordship's permission to have the last witness for the prosecution, Romaine Heilger, recalled.

(The CLERK rises and whispers to the JUDGE.)

JUDGE. When exactly, Sir Wilfrid, did this evidence come to your knowledge?

(The CLERK sits.)

SIR WILFRID. It was brought to me after the Court was adjourned last night.

MYERS. *(Rising)* My lord, I must object to my learned friend's request. The case for the prosecution is closed and . . .

(SIR WILFRID *sits.)*

JUDGE. Mr. Myers, I had not intended to rule on this question without first observing the customary formality of inviting your observations on the matter. Yes, Sir Wilfrid?

(MYERS *sits.)*

SIR WILFRID. *(Rising)* My lord, in a case where evidence vital to the prisoner comes into possession of his legal advisers at any time before the jury have returned their verdict, I contend that such evidence is not only admissable, but desirable. Happily there is clear authority to support my proposition, to be found in the case of the King against Stillman, reported in nineteen twenty-six

Appeal Cases at page four-six-three. *(He opens a law volume in front of him.)*

JUDGE. You needn't trouble to cite the authority, Sir Wilfrid, I am quite familiar with it. I should like to hear the prosecution. Now, Mr. Myers.

(SIR WILFRID *sits.)*

MYERS. *(Rising)* In my respectful submission, my lord, the course my friend proposes is, save in exceptional circumstances, quite unprecedented. And what, may I ask, is this startling new evidence of which Sir Wilfrid speaks?

SIR WILFRID. *(Rising)* Letters, my lord. Letters from Romaine Heilger.

JUDGE. I should like to see these letters to which you refer, Sir Wilfrid.

(SIR WILFRED *and* MYERS *sit. The* USHER *rises, crosses to* SIR WILFRID, *collects the letters, passes them to the* CLERK, *who hands them to the* JUDGE. *The* JUDGE *studies the letters. The* USHER *resumes his seat.)*

MYERS. *(Rising)* My friend was good enough to tell me only as we came into Court that he intended to make this submission, so that I have had no opportunity to examine the authorities. But I seem to remember a case in, I think, nineteen thirty, the King against Porter, I believe . . .

JUDGE. No, Mr. Myers, the King against Potter, and it was reported in nineteen thirty-one. I appeared for the prosecution.

MYERS. And if my memory serves me well, your lordship's similar objection was sustained.

JUDGE. Your memory for once serves you ill, Mr. Myers. My objection then was overruled by Mr. Justice Swindon—as yours is now, by me.

(MYERS *sits.*)

SIR WILFRID. *(Rising)* Call Romaine Heilger.

USHER. *(Rises and moves lown* C.) Romaine Heilger.

POLICEMAN. *(Opens the door. Calling)* Romaine Heilger.

JUDGE. If these letters are authentic it raises very serious issues. *(He hands the letters to the* CLERK.)

(The CLERK *hands the letters to the* USHER, *who returns them to* SIR WILFRID. *During the slight wait that ensues,* LEONARD *is very agitated. He speaks to the* WARDER, *then puts his hands to his face. The* USHER *sits on the stool* R. *of the table.* MAYHEW *rises, speaks to* LEONARD *and calms him down.* LEONARD *shakes his head and looks upset and worried.* ROMAINE *enters up* L., *crosses and enters the witness box. The* POLICEMAN *closes the door.)*

SIR WILFRID. Mrs. Heilger, you appreciate that you are still on your oath?

ROMAINE. Yes.

JUDGE. Romaine Heilger, you are recalled to this box so that Sir Wilfrid may ask you further questions.

SIR WILFRID. Mrs. Heilger, do you know a certain man whose Christian name is Max?

ROMAINE. *(Starts violently at the mention of the name.)* I don't know what you mean.

SIR WILFRID. *(Pleasantly.)* And yet it's a very simple question. Do you or do you not know a man called Max?

ROMAINE. Certainly not.

SIR WILFRID. You're quite sure of that?

ROMAINE. I've never known anyone called Max. Never.

SIR WILFRID. And yet I believe it's a fairly common Christian name, or contraction of a name, in your country. You mean that you have never known anyone of that name?

ROMAINE. *(Doubtfully.)* Oh, in Germany—yes—perhaps, I do not remember. It is a long time ago.

SIR WILFRID. I shall not ask you to throw your mind back such a long way as that. A few weeks will suffice. Let us say— *(He picks up one of the letters and unfolds it, making rather a parade of it.)* the seventeenth of October last.

ROMAINE. *(Startled.)* What have you got there?

SIR WILFRID. A letter.

ROMAINE. I don't know what you're talking about.

SIR WILFRID. I'm talking about a letter. A letter written on the seventeenth of October. You remember that date, perhaps.

ROMAINE. Not particularly, why?

SIR WILFRID. I suggest that on that day, you wrote a certain letter—a letter addressed to a man called Max.

ROMAINE. I did nothing of the kind. These are lies that you are telling. I don't know what you mean.

SIR WILFRID. That letter was one of a series written to the same man over a considerable period of time.

ROMAINE. *(Agitated.)* Lies—all lies!

SIR WILFRID. You would seem to have been on— *(Significantly.) intimate* terms with this man.

LEONARD. *(Rising)* How dare you say a thing like that?

(The WARDER *rises and attempts to restrain* LEONARD.*)*

(He waves the WARDER *aside.)* It isn't true!

JUDGE. The prisoner in his own interest will remain silent.

(LEONARD and the WARDER resume their seats.)

SIR WILFRID. I am not concerned with the general trend of this correspondence. I am only interested in one particular letter. *(He reads.)* "My beloved Max. An extraordinary thing has happened. I believe all our difficulties may be ended . . ."

ROMAINE. *(Interrupting in a frenzy)* It's a lie—I never wrote it. How did you get hold of that letter? Who gave it to you?

SIR WILFRID. How the letter came into my possession is irrelevant.

ROMAINE. You stole it. You are a thief as well as a liar. Or did some woman give it to you? Yes, I am right, am I not?

JUDGE. Kindly confine yourself to answering Counsel's questions.

ROMAINE. But I will not listen.

JUDGE. Proceed, Sir Wilfrid.

SIR WILFRID. So far you have only heard the opening phrases of the letter. Am I to understand that you definitely deny writing it?

ROMAINE. Of course I never wrote it. It is a forgery. It is an outrage that I should be forced to listen to a pack of lies—lies made up by a jealous woman.

SIR WILFRID. I suggest it is *you* who have lied. You have lied flagrantly and persistently in this Court and upon oath. And the reason *why* you have lied is made clear by— *(He taps the letter.)* this letter—written down by you in black and white.

ROMAINE. You are crazy. Why should I write down a lot of nonsense?

SIR WILFRID. Because a way had opened before you to freedom—and in planning to take that way, the fact that an innocent man would be sent to his death meant nothing to you. You have even included that final deadly touch of how you yourself managed accidently to wound Leonard Vole with a ham knife.

ROMAINE. *(Carried away with fury.)* I never wrote that. I wrote that he did it himself cutting the ham . . . *(Her voice dies away.)*

(All eyes in court turn on her.)

SIR WILFRID. *(Triumphantly.)* So you know what is in the letter—before I have read it.

ROMAINE. *(Casting aside all restraint)* Damn you! Damn you! Damn you!

LEONARD. *(Shouting)* Leave her alone. Don't bully her.

ROMAINE. *(Looking wildly around)* Let me get out of here—let me go. *(She comes out of the witness box.)*

(The USHER rises and restrains ROMAINE.)

JUDGE. Usher, give the witness a chair.
(ROMAINE *sinks on to the stool* R. *of the table, sobs hysterically and buries her face in her hands. The* USHER *crosses and sits on the stool down* R.)

Sir Wilfrid, will you now read the letter aloud so that the Jury can hear it.

SIR WILFRID. *(Reading)* "My beloved Max. An extraordinary thing has happened. I believe all our difficulties may be ended. I can come to you without any fear of endangering the valuable work you are doing in this country. The old lady I told you about has been murdered and I think Leonard is suspected. He was there earlier that night and his fingerprints will be all over the place. Nine-thirty seems to be the time. Leonard was home by then, but his alibi depends on me—on *me*. Supposing I say he came home much later and that he had blood on his clothes—he did have blood on his sleeve, because he cut his wrist at supper, so you see it would all fit in. I can even say he told me he killed her. Oh, Max, beloved! Tell me I can go ahead—it would be so wonderful to be free from playing the part of a loving, grateful wife. I know the Cause and the Party comes first, but if Leonard was convicted of murder, I could come to you safely and we could be together for always. Your adoring Romaine."

JUDGE. Romaine Heilger, will you go back into the witness box?
(ROMAINE *rises and enters the witness box.*)

You have heard that letter read. What have you to say?

ROMAINE. *(Frozen in defeat.)* Nothing.

LEONARD. Romaine, tell him you didn't write it. *I* know you didn't write it.

ROMAINE. *(Turning and fairly spitting out the words)* Of course I wrote it.

SIR WILFRID. That, my lord, concludes the case for the defence.

JUDGE. Sir Wilfrid, have you any evidence as to whom these letters were addressed?

SIR WILFRID. My lord, they came into my possession anonymously, and there has been as yet no time to ascertain any further facts. It would seem likely that he came to this country illegally and is engaged on some subversive operations here . . .

ROMAINE. You will never find out who he is—never. I don't care what you do to me. You shall never know.

JUDGE. Do you wish to re-examine, Mr. Myers?

(SIR WILFRID *sits.*)

MYERS. *(Rising rather unhappily)* Really, my lord, I find it somewhat difficult in view of these startling developments. *(To* ROMAINE.*)* Mrs. Heilger, you are, I think, of a highly nervous temperament. Being a foreigner you may not quite realize the responsibilities that lie upon you when you take the oath in an English court of law. If you have been intimidated into admitting something that is not true, if you wrote a letter under stress or in some spirit of make-believe, do not hesitate to say so now.

ROMAINE. Must you go on and on torturing me? I wrote the letter. Now let me go.

MYERS. My lord, I submit that this witness is in such a state of agitation that she hardly knows what she is saying or admitting.

JUDGE. You may remember, Mr. Myers, that Sir Wilfrid cautioned the witness at the time of her previous statement and impressed upon her the sacred nature of the oath she had taken.

(MYERS *sits.*)

Mrs. Heilger, I wish to warn you that this is not the end of the matter. In this country you cannot commit perjury without being brought to account for it, and I may tell you that I have no doubt proceedings for perjury will shortly be taken against you. The sentence for perjury can be severe. You may stand down.

> (ROMAINE *stands down. The* POLICEMAN *opens the door.* ROMAINE *crosses and exits. The* POLICEMAN *closes the door.)*

Sir Wilfrid, will you now address the Jury on behalf of the defence?

SIR WILFRID. *(Rising)* Members of the Jury, when truth is clearly evident it speaks for itself. No words of mine I'm sure can add to the impression made upon you by the straightforward story which the prisoner has told, and by the very wicked attempt to incriminate him, evidence of which you have just witnessed . . .

> *(As* SIR WILFRID *speaks the LIGHTS dim to black-out. After a few seconds the LIGHTS come up. The* JURY *are out but are just re-entering the box.)*

CLERK. *(Rising)* Vole, stand up.

> (LEONARD *rises.)*

Members of the Jury, are you all agreed upon your verdict?

FOREMAN. *(Standing)* We are.

CLERK. Do you find the prisoner, Leonard Vole, guilty or not guilty?

FOREMAN. Not guilty, my lord.

> *(A buzz of approbation goes round the court.)*

USHER. *(Rising and moving down* C.) Silence!

JUDGE. Leonard Vole, you have been found not guilty of the murder of Emily French on October fourteenth. You are hereby discharged and are free to leave the Court. *(He rises.)*

> (ALL *rise. The* JUDGE *bows to the Court and exits up* R., *followed by the* ALDERMAN *and the* JUDGE'S CLERK.)

USHER. All persons who have anything further to do

before my lady the Queen's justices of Oyer and Terminer and general gaol delivery for the jurisdiction of the Central Criminal Court may depart hence and give your attendance here again tomorrow morning at ten-thirty o'clock. God Save The Queen.

(The USHER, *the* JURY *and the* STENOGRAPHER *exit down* R. *The* BARRISTERS, ASSISTANTS *and the* CLERK OF THE COURT *exit up* C. *The* WARDER *and the* POLICEMAN *exit up* L. LEONARD *leaves the dock and crosses to* MAYHEW.)

MAYHEW. Congratulations, my boy!
LEONARD. I can't thank you enough.
MAYHEW. *(Tactfully indicating* SIR WILFRID) This is the man you've got to thank.

(LEONARD *crosses to* C. *to meet* SIR WILFRID, *but comes face to face with* MYERS, *who glares at him, and exits up* C. SIR WILFRID *crosses to* R. *of* LEONARD.)

LEONARD. *(Turning to* SIR WILFRID) Thank you, sir. *(His tone is less spontaneous than it was to* MAYHEW. *He dislikes* SIR WILFRID *it seems.)* You—you've got me out of a very nasty mess.
SIR WILFRID. Nasty mess! Do you hear that, John? Your troubles are over now, my boy.
MAYHEW. *(Moving to* L. *of* LEONARD) But it was a near thing, you know.
LEONARD. *(Unwillingly.)* Yes, I suppose it was.
SIR WILFRID. If we hadn't been able to break that woman down . . .
LEONARD. Did you have to go for her the way you did? It was terrible the way she went to pieces. I can't believe . . .
SIR WILFRID. *(With all the force of his personality.)* Look here, Vole, you're not the first young man I've known who's been so crazy over a woman that he's been

blinded to what she's really like. That woman did her level best to put a rope round your neck.

MAYHEW. And don't you forget it.

LEONARD. Yes, but why? I can't see why. She's always seemed so devoted. I could have sworn she loved me—and yet all the time she was going with this other fellow. *(He shakes his head.)* It's unbelievable—there's something there I don't understand.

WARDER. *(Enters up L. and moves to L. of the table.)* Just two or three minutes more, sir. We'll slip you out to a car by the side entrance.

LEONARD. Is there still a crowd?

(ROMAINE, *escorted by the* POLICEMAN, *enters up* L.)

POLICEMAN. *(In the doorway.)* Better wait in here, ma'am. The crowd's in a nasty mood. I'd let them disperse before you try to leave.

ROMAINE. *(Moving down* L. *of the table)* Thank you.

(The POLICEMAN *and the* WARDER *exit up* L. ROMAINE *crosses towards* LEONARD.)

SIR WILFRID. *(Intercepting* ROMAINE) No, you don't.

ROMAINE. *(Amused.)* Are you protecting Leonard from me? Really, there's no need.

SIR WILFRID. You've done enough harm.

ROMAINE. Mayn't I even congratulate Leonard on being free?

SIR WILFRID. No thanks to you.

ROMAINE. And rich.

LEONARD. *(Uncertainly.)* Rich?

MAYHEW. Yes, I think,, Mr. Vole, that you will certainly inherit a great deal of money.

LEONARD. *(Boyishly.)* Money doesn't seem to mean so much after what I've been through. Romaine, I can't understand . . .

ROMAINE. *(Smoothly.)* Leonard, I can explain.

SIR WILFRID. No!

(SIR WILFRID *and* ROMAINE *look at each other like antagonists.*)

ROMAINE. Tell me, do those words the Judge said mean that I shall—go to prison?

SIR WILFRID. You will quite certainly be charged with perjury and tried for it. You will probably go to prison.

LEONARD. *(Awkwardly.)* I'm sure that—that everything will come right. Romaine, don't worry.

MAYHEW. Will you never see sense, Vole? Now we must consider practicalities—this matter of probate.

(MAYHEW *draws* LEONARD *down* R., *where they murmur together.* SIR WILFRID *and* ROMAINE *remain, measuring each other.*)

SIR WILFRID. It may interest you to know that I took your measure the first time we met. I made up my mind then to beat you at your little game, and by God I've done it. I've got him off—in spite of you.

ROMAINE. In *spite*—of me.

SIR WILFRID. You don't deny, do you, that you did your best to hang him?

ROMAINE. Would they have believed me if I had said that he was at home with me that night, and did not go out? Would they?

SIR WILFRID. *(Slightly uncomfortable.)* Why not?

ROMAINE. Because they would have said to themselves: this woman loves this man—she would say or do anything for him. They would have had sympathy with me, yes. But they would not have *believed* me.

SIR WILFRID. If you'd been speaking the truth they would.

ROMAINE. I wonder. *(She pauses.)* I did not want their sympathy—I wanted them to dislike me, to mistrust me, to be convinced that I was a liar. And then, when my lies were broken down—then they believed . . . *(In the Cockney accent of the* WOMAN *who visited* SIR WILFRID

at his office.) So now you know the whole story, mister—
like to kiss me?

SIR WILFRID. *(Thunderstruck.)* My God!

ROMAINE. *(As herself.)* Yes, the woman with the letters. I wrote those letters. I brought them to you. I was
that woman. It wasn't *you* who won freedom for Leonard.
It was *I*. And because of it I shall go to prison. *(Her eyes
close.)* But at the end of it Leonard and I will be together again. Happy—loving each other.

SIR WILFRID. *(Moved.)* My dear . . . But couldn't
you trust me? We believe, you know, that our British
system of justice upholds the truth. We'd have got him
off.

ROMAINE. I couldn't risk it. *(Slowly.)* You see, you
thought he was innocent . . .

SIR WILFRID. *(With quick appreciation.)* And you
knew he was innocent. I understand.

ROMAINE. But you do not understand at all. *I* knew he
was *guilty*.

SIR WILFRID. *(Thunderstruck.)* But aren't you afraid?

ROMAINE. Afraid?

SIR WILFRID. Of linking your life with a murderer's.

ROMAINE. You don't understand—we love each other.

SIR WILFRID. The first time I met you I said you were
a vrey remarkable woman—I see no reason to change my
opinion. *(Crosses and exits up* C.)

WARDER. *(Off up* L.) It's no good going in there, miss.
It's all over.

(There is a COMMOTION off up L. *and then a* GIRL
comes running on up L. *She is a very young strawberry blonde with a crude, obvious appeal. She
rushes to* LEONARD *through the Q.C.'s bench and
meets him down* R.C.)

GIRL. Len, darling, you're free. *(She embraces him.)*
Isn't it wonderful? They're trying to keep me out. Darling, it's been awful. I've been nearly crazy.

ROMAINE. *(With sudden violent harshness.)* Leonard
—who—is—this girl!

GIRL. *(To* ROMAINE, *defiantly.)* I'm Len's girl. I know
all about *you.* You're not his wife. Never have been. *(She
crosses to* R. *of* ROMAINE.) You're years older than him,
and you just got hold of him—and you've done your best
to hang him. But that's all over now. *(She turns to*
LEONARD.) We'll go abroad like you said on one of your
cruises—to all those grand places. We'll have a wonderful time.

ROMAINE. Is—this—true? Is she your girl, Leonard?

LEONARD. *(Hesitates, then decides that the situation
must be accepted.)* Yes, she is.

(The GIRL *crosses above* LEONARD *to* R. *of him.)*

ROMAINE. After all I've done for you . . . What can
she do for you that can compare with that?

LEONARD. *(Flinging off all disguise of manner, and
showing coarse brutality.)* She's fifteen years younger
than you are. *(He laughs.)*

*(*ROMAINE *flinches as though struck.)*
(He crosses to R. *of* ROMAINE. *Menacingly.)* I've got the
money. I've been acquitted, and I can't be tried again,
so don't go shooting off your mouth, or you'll just get
yourself hanged as an accessory after the fact. *(He turns
to the* GIRL *and embraces her.)*

ROMAINE. *(Picks up the knife from the table. Throw-
ing her head back in sudden dignity.)* No, that will not
happen. I shall not be tried as an accessory after the fact.
I shall not be tried for perjury. I shall be tried for murder— *(She stabs* LEONARD *in the back.)* the murder of
the only man I ever loved.

*(*LEONARD *drops. The* GIRL *screams.* MAYHEW *bends
over* LEONARD, *feels his pulse and shakes his head.)*
(She looks up at the JUDGE'S *seat.)* Guilty, my lord.

CURTAIN

WITNESS FOR THE PROSECUTION

FURNITURE AND PROPERTY PLOT

ACT ONE

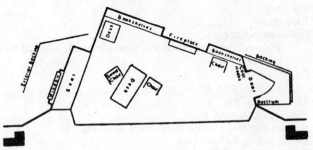

On stage
Bookcases
In them:
    Legal volumes
On them:
    Deed-boxes, books
Tall reading desk
On it:
    Books
Desk
On it:
    Angle-poise desk lamp, telephone, botter, inkstand,
    pens, pencils, ashtray, legal documents, books, paper
    knife
In desk drawer:
    Empty matchbox, cigarettes

Under desk:
   Books
Swivel chair
2 upright chairs
Waste-paper basket
Coal scuttle
Carpet on floor
Window curtains
On window seat:
   Cushion, deed-box, box-file, legal documents
Fender
Fire-irons
On mantelpiece:
   Tobacco jar with tobacco, pipe cleaners, box-file with
   papers
Over mantelpiece:
   Picture, clip with papers
Mirror (on wall R.)
Pictures (on wall R.)
2 pairs electric candle-lamp wall-brackets
Light switch below door
Bell push L. of fireplace
Coat-hooks on wall above door

   Off stage
Letters (CARTER)
Nail varnish and brush (GRETA)
Brief-case
In it:
   Documents (MAYHEW)
SIR WILFRID's jacket and bow (CARTER)
Wig and gown (SIR WILFRID)
Evening paper (GRETA)

   Personal
CARTER: watch
MAYHEW: pipe
SIR WILFRID: empty matchbox

ACT TWO

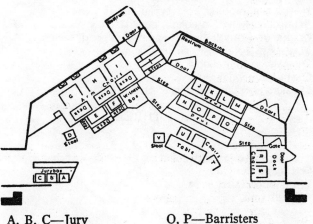

A, B, C—Jury
D—Court Usher
E—Clerk of the Court
F—Court Stenographer
G—Judge's Clerk
H—Judge
I—Alderman
J, K, L, M—Barristers
N—Mr. Myers, Q.C.

O, P—Barristers
Q—Sir Wilfrid Robarts, Q.C.
R—Warder
S—Leonard Vole
T—Mr. Mayhew
U—Inspector
V—Doctor

On stage
Built-in seats and desks
3 armchairs
5 chairs
2 stools
Table. *On it:* exhibits, knife, will, jacket
On witness box: oath card, Bible
On jury box: oath card, Bible
In dock: pencil, notepad
On Judge's desk: books, papers, notepad, pencil
On Barristers' desks: books, papers, notepads, pencils

Personal
SIR WILFRID: blood donor certificate
INSPECTOR: notebook, 2 typed sheets
STENOGRAPHER: Notebook, pencil
CLERK OF COURT: books, papers, notepad, pencil
MAYHEW: brief-case. *In it:* documents
DR. WYATT: notebook
CLEGG: notebook
MYERS: German marriage certificate

ACT THREE

SCENE I

Setting as Act One
Window curtains open
All lights off

Off stage
Brief-case (MAYHEW)
Tray. *On it:* 2 cups of tea (GRETA)

Personal
SIR WILFRID: handkerchief, wallet. *In it:* £5 note
MAYHEW: pipe, wallet. *In it:* £20 in notes
WOMAN: handbag. *In it:* letters

SCENE II

Setting as Act Two
Exchange knife on table for trick knife
Personal
SIR WILFRID: letters, law volume

WITNESS FOR THE PROSECUTION

LIGHTING PLOT

ACT ONE

Property fittings required:
> 2 pairs electric candle-lamp wall-brackets (practical)
> Angle-poise desk lamp (practical)
> Light switch below door L.

Interior. Afternoon
The apparent sources of light are, in daytime a window
R.; at night, wall-brackets R. and L. of the fireplace
up C. and an angle-poise lamp on the desk R.C.
The main acting areas are R.C. and C.
To open: Effect of afternoon sunshine
No cues

ACT TWO

Property fittings required—none
Interior. Morning
The apparent source of light is from windows presumed
to be in the "fourth wall"
The main acting areas are R.C., C., L.C. and L.
To open: Effect of morning sunshine
No cues

ACT THREE

SCENE I

Setting as Act One. Night

III

To open:
  Blue outside window
  Stage lights out
  Wall-brackets out
  Desk lamp out

Cue 1:
  SIR WILFRID switches on wall-brackets
  Bring up lights to cover c. stage
  Switch on wall-brackets

Cue 2:
  SIR WILFRID switches on desk lamp
  Bring up lights to cover R.C.
  Switch on desk lamp

SCENE II

Setting as Act Two
To open: Effect of morning sunshine
Cue 3:
  SIR WILFRID: . . . you have just witnessed.
  Quick dim of all lights to black-out, hold for 8 seconds, then return to opening lighting